Golden Wings and Other Stories about Birders and Birding

Golden

and Other Stories

Pete Dunne

Wings

about Birders and Birding

UNIVERSITY OF TEXAS PRESS, AUSTIN

Printed in the United States of America

First edition, 2003

∞ The paper used in this book meets the minimum requirements of ANSI/NISO Z39.48-1992 (R1997) (Permanence of Paper).

Library of Congress Cataloging-in-Publication Data

Dunne, Pete, 1951–
Golden wings and other stories about birders and birding / Pete Dunne.
p. cm. — (The Corrie Herring Hooks series ; no. 56)
ISBN 0-292-71621-4 (cloth : alk. paper) —
ISBN 0-292-71623-0 (pbk. : alk. paper)
1. Bird watchers—anecdotes. 2. Bird watching—Anecdotes. I. Title. II. Series.
QL677.5.D853 2003
598'.07'234—dc21

2002011187

Earlier versions of these essays appeared in Pete Dunne's columns "The Catbird Seat" in *Living Bird* (1986–2002) and "Beak to Tale" in *Wild Bird News* (1996–2002).

Corrie Herring Hooks Series,
Number Fifty-Six

This book is dedicated to *Virginia Marie Peterson*
For friendship and things held in trust

Contents

Acknowledgments

As a reader, you have now become a partner in this book. Accordingly, I want to invite your indulgence and ask that you join me in recognizing the following individuals and institutions who were, in some way, instrumental in these writings.

Principal among them are editors Tim Gallagher of the Cornell Laboratory of Ornithology's quarterly, *Living Bird*; Jane Crowley of *Wild Bird News*; Fletcher Roberts of the New Jersey Sunday section, the *New York Times*; Eldon Greij, founding editor of *Birder's World*; and Sandy Sherman whose red pen falls frequently and at need upon the pages of the *Kestrel Express* and *Peregrine Observer*, the publications of New Jersey Audubon Society's Cape May Bird Observatory.

Collections of essays are not commonly best-sellers. It takes a special kind of publishing house to take them seriously. In this respect, University of Texas Press is second to none. They have made the publishing of this collection and the four that preceded it as much fun to execute as to write. My thanks to them, all of them, in the most collective sense.

Finally and once again, my very heartfelt thanks to my friend Dorothy Clair whose editorial skills do her and the trade proud (and make me look like a much better writer than I am).

Preface

Collections of essays are always something of a chimera. A little of this, a little of that. Add a dash of whimsy, stir in some insight, and add a pinch of pique. If a writer is lucky, what ultimately gets wrapped between hard covers doesn't turn out half bad, might even (if the writer is uncommonly lucky) seem thematically knit.

I don't know why, but this, my fifth collection of essays, was that lucky. In fact, the essays don't just knit. In their order and expression, they seem almost to have been written in concert.

How could this be? Well, it's certainly not through any conscious design. They were written over an eight-year period and culled from many scores of essays. One day I printed out my finalists, spread them out on the office floor, and, perusing the titles, assembled them in an order that seemed workable. They never got the benefit of a second thought or even a shuffling of the deck.

Only now do I realize that my hand must have been guided by some *un*conscious design, some writer's sixth sense. There is an order that goes with the arranging of these essays and a purpose, too. But what that is you'll have to discover for yourself. If you fail, don't worry. Essays are written to stand on their own. One birder to another, I'm confident you'll enjoy these. They deal with subjects to which you and I can easily relate.

The elements of this collection were drawn from an assortment of columns that I have written and, in some cases, continue to write. The two that offered the most material were "The Catbird Seat" from *Living Bird*, a quarterly published by the Cornell Laboratory of Ornithology, and "Birding Beak to Tale" (sponsored by Swarovski Optik of North America), my column in *Wild Bird News*, the newsletter of the Wild Bird Centers store chain. Other sources include "The Natural State," a column I wrote for the New Jersey Sunday section of the *New York Times*; the *Peregrine Observer* (journal of the New Jersey Audubon Society's Cape May Bird Observatory); *Kestrel Express* (CMBO's quarterly newsletter); and "Birder at Large," at one time, a regular feature in *Birder's World*. Of these sources, only "Birding Beak to Tale" and "Birder at Large" might be said to have thematic kinship. The rest had a focus or theme that was distinct (except, of course, for the universal focus upon birds). Some were written to engage a serious birding audience; others were written for more casual, backyard birders (*even nonbirders* in the case of the *New York Times* column).

Some were meant to provoke, some to amuse; some were caustic, some instructional, some nostalgic; some were flights of fancy. As a writer, I like to let my imagination run and see where it goes. One of the places it went was the title essay of this collection, "Golden Wings." A real anomaly, this one. A story written to be read aloud at the banquet of the American Birding Association in Tucson, Arizona, in 1999. Since that first reading, I've presented it at various festivals and forums and delighted in every telling. It's a story that pays tribute to a great and wonderful man, someone who was for too short a time in our respective lives, a friend, a mentor . . . and maybe something of a father figure, too. I was, he confided to me (and wife Ginny many times recalled), one of his "adopted sons." Putting this story in print is my way of paying tribute, and saying thank you, to a man who inspired me and many others.

His name, by the way, was Roger Tory Peterson. I'll bet you've heard of him. But you may not have heard of Ginny. Mrs. Peterson to some, Virginia Marie Peterson to others. Until his death on July 28, 1996, she was the wife of Roger Tory Peterson. Until her death, on Easter Sunday, 2001, she remained his greatest champion.

We met the day I met her famous husband. It was the eve of the first World Series of Birding—Friday, May 17, 1984. Roger, at age seventy-six, was to be a teammate on that first twenty-four-hour birding competition. Ginny was there to insure that the safety of the world's greatest naturalist (not to mention her husband) was not jeopardized.

I'm seeing it happen again as I write: Roger stepping from the train and onto the platform of the train station in Newark, New Jersey. He and I shaking hands, smiling; two born truants on the eve of adventure. Only then did I reach for the hand of the golden-haired woman who stood like a guardian angel over Roger's right shoulder. Her eyes damn near pinned me to the pavement.

Strange to say, I cannot recall the color of those eyes. But if described on some color chart in a paint store, "no-nonsense cool" would not be inappropriate. Looking into them, I think I understood better the woman who'd written out a *three-page, single-spaced* set of pre–World Series instructions for me: no-nonsense "dos" and "don'ts" regarding Roger and his needs. We'd also spent no small amount of time on the phone—Ginny making sure I understood the significance of my charge, me assuring her that I did.

I'm not going to say that Ginny's trainstation appraisal inspired her instant trust. But something she saw must have reassured her, because she smiled—a smile that unfolded like a butterfly but had the quality of a firefly cupped secretly in a child's hands. She loved both butterflies and secrets. Even the cancer that metamorphosed within her, turning body into spirit, was a secret known only to a few.

Of course, she had accomplishments of her own. But it was as principal cartographer on the maps of both the *Eastern Birds* and *Western Birds* guides that her talents were brought to bear on birding. When she and Roger did book signings, she signed only the maps. When Roger died, leaving the future of the unfinished fifth edition of his *Eastern Birds* hanging in the balance, it was Ginny who picked up the reins to see the project through.

As a writer, I can tell you that it is the last five percent of any writing project that is the hardest, and often it is only the momentum of writing that carries a project to completion. From a cold start, Ginny faced a book that was only eighty percent finished. She brought her organizational skills to bear and mustered a team of experts. Under her direction, fueled by her energy and commitment, they completed their task.

When Ginny died, the complete text and finished plates were in the hands of Houghton Mifflin Company. Now published, the fifth edition of Peterson's *Eastern Birds* is as much a tribute to her spirit as it is the legacy of her husband.

She was a warm and wonderful person, Ginny—a woman whose strengths could, and did, balance the gravitational pull of a star. It should come as no surprise, therefore, that this collection is dedicated to her.

Pete Dunne
New Jersey Audobon Society's Cape May Bird Observatory
Goshen, New Jersey

Golden Wings and Other Stories about Birders and Birding

Eye of the Beheld

"Hello," I said softly, because what I had to say was personal and because there was no need to shout across the short span that separated us. "You are beautiful."

As opening lines go, this one isn't very original, but it was apt. The bird *was* beautiful, overwhelmingly actually. Set like a black-and-white cloud atop a pedestal nest, eight-inch bill cocked demurely down, fathomless dark eyes locked with mine, I was prepared to assert (even to wife Linda who was not far away and burning film) that the Wandering Albatross was the most beautiful thing I'd ever seen.

What the bird was thinking is anyone's guess. But it was clear that she was not discomfited by my proximity—in fact, it was her serenity, as much as her beauty, that invited communion. And I had come a long way for this moment. Not geographically. The distance between Cape May, New Jersey, and the island of South Georgia is only half my annual commute. Not in evolutionary terms, either. By divergent paths, all creatures on this planet have reached this point in time and space in a tie. No, the distance I'd traveled to see this bird is measured in the span of a human life, my life. I was close enough to see my reflection in the eye of one of the planet's most celebrated birds, and I was having trouble accommodating this.

"It's like this," I said, to my reflection. "There was this kid growing up in Whippany, New Jersey, and in time he grew up to be you. By the way," I added for the benefit of the bird, "Whippany's about 30 miles west of New York City." While Wandering Albatross aren't called "wandering" for nothing, their grasp of geography in the northern hemisphere is patchy.

"This kid," I continued, "really liked birds. But being a kid, and being unable to travel, he had a tempered notion about what birds he was likely to see in his life and what birds were just plain out of reach."

The reflection, being a reflection, said nothing. The bird, being a bird, didn't respond.

"He looked in books at things like Red-faced Warblers and Tawny Frogmouths and thought of how neat it would be to see birds like that, but he figured he never would."

Neither the reflection nor the bird gave any evidence that they grasped the point—so I showed them.

"Well, you saw your first Red-faced Warbler in 1986," I confided. "Tawny Frogmouth in 1987. You were wrong, Dunne. Lucky and wrong but. . . "

"But you never dreamed you'd see this did, you?" I said first to the reflection and then to the person whose reflection was being reflected upon. And this was really the heart of it, the cognitive impasse. In all my imaginings, I'd never even dreamed this dream to even deny it.

Dream or deny that someday I would be sitting on a grassy knoll on the island of South Georgia and seeing my life reflected in the eye of one of this planet's most marvelous birds. It was and remains a privilege almost beyond bearing and a tribute to an avocation that can ferry its proponents to every corner of the globe.

"Thank you," I said, to the bird, and to the fortune that guides lives. Then, finding nothing else to say, and finding no better way of expressing it than honoring the bird's peace, I set off to find Linda. To share with her this moment. To tell her of the wonder and beauty I'd found not in the eye of the beholder but, unlooked for, in eye of the beheld.

All You Need Is $

"I think I'd like to try birding," my sister-in-law, Lindsay, observed the other day. "What do I need to get started?"

"That's wonderful," I chirped. Everyone loves it when someone affirms your choice of avocations by inviting their inclusion. My mouth twisted to offer the usual, banal reply: "All you need are binoculars and a field guide," but this time the words refused to glide from my lips.

"This," some surviving shred of human decency screamed in my mind, "is my sister-in-law. Someone I love. Someone to whom I am accountable."

Someone who could back me into a corner in front of parents and siblings and read me the riot act when the ugly truth behind the fair cloak of this foul lie is laid bare.

Lie? Yes, lie. You and I both know "binoculars and a field guide" are *not* the only things you need to go birding. These items are just the down payment. The real cost, measured in the currency of material goods and social compromise, could bankrupt you.

Don't I love it when an incipient birder calls and asks where they can go to test a number of different binocular makes and models before buying?

"Oh, that's easy," I reply. "Just look up any birder." All birder's have a bottom drawer filled with binoculars that they don't use anymore—instruments bought and retired as their owners climbed the ladder to the optical top of the chart.

As for " . . . and a field guide," well, I think a prerequisite for any new birder should be: room in the basement. This will serve as storage space for all the literary classics, book-of-the-month club offerings, and self-help books that your future library of general field guides, specialty field guides, and bird-finding guides is destined to displace.

"All you need. . . " says nothing about the stacks of periodicals you'll be forced to subscribe to—to keep up with the latest species splits and to learn where you (and the family) are going for your next vacation.

"Mommy, where's the Salton Sea?"

"California, darling. *Shhh,* Mommy's trying to decide how many field guides to bring."

It doesn't address the need for outerwear that will prove too warm for Big Bend in June, and too light for Newburyport in February, and whose pocket deficiency will force you to trade in your sedan for a sport-utility vehicle—so you will have room for the traveling birding library as well as the scope and tripod that was also never mentioned by that person who told you "all you need is . . . "

"Binoculars and a field guide!" Oh, that banal lie, that poisonous, budget-busting tantalization. It is only a matter of weeks, *days,* before the average incipient birder muses: "If I just had a camera, I could take pictures of birds myself!"

Camera leads to lens. Lens leads to lenses and telephoto flash systems and multiple camera bodies. Take it from someone who once bought a 600mm telephoto lens instead of a house. No matter how many thousands of dollars you spend on camera equipment, you *never* have the right equipment for the occasion (even after you buy it).

But you're a birder. You know this.

You also know what happened to your circle of friends after the catalytic addition of "binoculars and a field guide" to your life. How old acquaintances who once enlivened dinner parties with discussions of "impeachable offenses," and "finest exhibit of modern impressionism I've ever seen" moved out, and people who argue, tirelessly, about "arrested molt sequence" and "photo vs. illustrated field guides" moved in.

How a telephone call received at 5:30 A.M. now constitutes normal behavior, and calls received after 8:30 P.M. are greeted with a snarl.

How when commuting distance was assessed as a factor governing the location of your new home, the reference point wasn't "workplace" or "surviving parent," it was distance to "nearest migrant trap."

I thought of all of these things, as my mouth remained slack, as my sister-in-law waited, and I could not avoid thinking about the inevitable social costs that a life of birding places on family members, too. On children! Nieces and nephews who in their efforts to garner pledges for walkathons in support of the senior class trip are destined to find that Mom beat them to aunts and uncles to get support for her Big Sit. On brother Dave, Lindsay's husband, who used to beat me up regularly (for no greater offense than using the last of the milk on my cereal) and who once observed: "*You mean that there's a six o'clock in the morning, too?!*" I thought . . .

You know that all of these social and financial ramifications are just too complicated to try to explain (even to a much-loved sister-in-law). Besides, I've always wanted to get back at my brother Dave.

"All you need are binoculars and a field guide," I heard myself saying through a smile. "Your life will never be the same."

Directions, Please!

Birding is a source of extreme gratification—but the cause of considerable frustration, too. There are binoculars that will not focus at a short enough distance, field guides that never depict the birds you find, and fellow birders eager to tell you about the bird you didn't find.

"You just missed it."

"Really."

"Flew when you turned the corner."

"Really."

"I've waited thirty years to see one."

"Really. Forty, in my case."

But the greatest frustration a birder can be frustrated by is not the bird you missed, not the bird that has eluded you for "forty years," but the one you can't find RIGHT NOW (because some direction-challenged companion cannot get you on the bird).

How many times have you stood there, strangling with anxiety—a Life Bird/Year Bird/Good Bird hanging in the balance—and had some well-intentioned soul/fellow birder chirp, "It's right in front of you."

I don't know about you, but I find the area "right in front of me" to be a very big place (encompassing about half the known universe). Somehow it is always my fortune to fall in with people who couldn't direct a compass needle to magnetic north and whose sense of refining detail is as discriminating as gravity.

What do I mean by this?

I mean that, in response to my next controlled observation: "I don't see it," they will invariably reply: "It's in the tree."

I have learned to stop all inquiries at this point. Further inquiry only confirms that the tree they are referring to is, of course, "the tree right in front of us."

"The one standing in the spruce forest?"

"Yes. That tree."

However, sometimes the birds I can't find are in clouds, not trees, and sometimes it is my fortune to be with people who are *too* specific to be helpful—people who can't see the forest for the four-sided needles or the alto cumulus for thc water vapor.

I recall an occasion when a well-traveled companion tried to get me on some fast-retiring raptorial speck in a cloud-filled sky.

"Do you see the cloud shaped like Ecuador?"

"Ecuador?"

"Well, the bird is in Quito."

"Where the hell is Quito?"

"Uh . . . forget it. The cloud just changed into Venezuela and the bird's leaving Caracas for the States."

I don't have any greater fortune finding seabirds (or choosing sea-birding companions). Here's another drama in which I once played a subordinate role.

"I've got a Gannet."

"Where?"

"On the horizon. One o'clock. Going right."

"Don't have it."

"Two o'clock."

"Don't have it."

"Now going left again. One o'clock.

"Don't have it."

"Twelve o'clock . . . 11:45 . . . 11:40 . . . "

"A.M. or P.M.?"

OK, so maybe I'm just not good at finding birds. And maybe I should be grateful. Because finding birds and getting people on them sets up a whole 'nother problem—like accountability. What if your identification is wrong?

Here's a story about a bird-finding exercise that went right . . .

then wrong. It involved two tour leaders (who will remain anonymous).

"Gyrfalcon!" the first leader exclaimed.

"Where? Where?" the group chanted.

"In the scope," the leader replied.

All participants got their look. Then the other leader got his turn.

"I don't see it," he said, after pensive study.

Surprised, the first leader looked again and announced, "It's right in the center of the scope."

Respectfully, the second leader peered into the scope again only to repeat, "I don't see *the Gyrfalcon*."

Exasperated, the first leader commandeered the scope and looked again. "It's dead center," he insisted.

Like a general sending troops into a battle that cannot be won, like a judge sentencing a friend for crimes that do not warrant punishment, the second leader returned to the scope, peered down the barrel, sighed, and asked, "Where is the Gyrfalcon relative to the Snow Bunting?"

Now if only I'd been second leader on this trip, there wouldn't have been a problem.

Or a story.

Listening with Longing, Settling for Beauty

The sound became too loud to ignore and it finally brought my head up. The sound of Canada Geese. They were already close . . . and closing. They passed directly overhead.

Maybe it was the proximity that brought my awareness to bear. Maybe it was the magical sound of wind through slotted wings that brought back some of that old-time feeling, or perhaps the sheer volume of their cry ignited my attention.

For whatever reason, I realized, suddenly, that the birds were beautiful and their passage haunting. I found this thought strange and disquietingly sad because, like most people, I get to ignore Canada Geese every day.

This wasn't always the case, of course. Once, even the rumor of distant dogs barking would root me in my tracks and draw my eyes to the sky. A wedged flock passing overhead would prompt strangers on street corners to pause in their hurry and trade nods and smiles as if something special had been shared.

And it was special.

Aldo Leopold's greatest verse would be inspired by that haunting sound, and Roger Tory Peterson would dedicate one of his precious "Dozen Birding Hotspots" to a refuge whose claim to fame was that of goose factory.

And in the night. When the cries of wild geese would slip through open windows and pry you from sleep. Don't you remember how that sound beat a resonate tattoo on the place that lies just below the ribs—the place where human longing is stored? Didn't you feel your soul spread its wings and join the passage birds in spirit? Wasn't that the way it was?

Before game management engineers staged a spectacular goose population boom? Before wasteful agricultural practices produced a bounty of grain to fuel wintering flocks? Before a landscaping penchant that turns forest into the habitat equivalent of affordable housing for Canada Geese came to dominate the landscape?

Before geese became the bane of golfers, a blight on corporate lawns, and so numerous that national refuges can't even give the birds away? Before one of the most magical sounds in the world, the sound of Canada Geese, was diminished by repetition and volume?

I feel like I do when in an elevator I hear some catchy tune that I really liked the first sixty or eighty times I heard it but can't abide now.

I feel like Midas, surrounded by gold, who wants only to savor, once again, the remembered taste of wine on his tongue.

I want to be pried from sleep, as I used to be, by the cry—slipping through the window—of geese. I want to feel the dimly remembered hunger for things that have not yet been, experience the wings-wide reach for the distant horizon and whatever fortune lies there for the taking.

But if I cannot have these things because there is not enough magic left in the world or because the having has dulled the longing, then I will settle for this: that every once in a while, a flock of geese will pass close enough to cut through the commonplace and turn my head so that I will see them and say, "They are beautiful."

Birding Tough

He was big and quiet and staring out the window. He was wearing a jacket whose sleeves reached just below the elbows, and a look that betrayed his unease.

"This guy is as big as a dump truck," I thought.

"Congratulations on winning this year's Conservationist of the Year award," I said. "You Barnegat Baymen sure deserve it."

"Thank you," he intoned, taking my hand in a weathered paw that looked to be about the size and texture of a first-baseman's glove. "You birders are nice to recognize us this way."

There followed a moment of silence that became a period of silence that became an embarrassment to us both. Fact was, I just didn't know how to go about having a conversation with a guy who looked like he amused himself by sparring with Grizzly Bears.

I've seen these baymen before, of course, while scanning for winter raptors out over coastal marshes—Rough-legged Hawks that hover and Short-eared Owls that float like giant moths—*seen* these weather-hardened individuals standing up to their waists in the backwaters of Barnegat Bay. Stripped down to T-shirts. Fully exposed to the wind. Working clam rakes in water so cold it would freeze an eider.

Me? I'm just a birder. Like to stay warm; like to stay dry. I have a spotting scope that lets me scan all the way to the horizon (so I don't have to go there) and a graphite tripod that's so light I *could* carry it all the way to the horizon. Should I choose. Which I don't. If the horizon is where I want to be, I drive there. Take the scope off the tripod. Put it on a window mount. Drive to a strategic vantage point. Do my scanning from the comfort of my car.

But these Barnegat Baymen were something else again. "You'd have to be an animal to stand out there and take cold like that," I'd more than once mused. "You'd have to be . . . "

"Boy," he said, breaking the silence. "You birders are sure tough."

"Excuse me?" I said.

"I said you birders are *tough*," he replied again, shaking his great head for emphasis.

"How do you figure?" I asked.

"Aw, we see you people out there," he admitted. "Standing out in those marshes in the dead of winter, scanning for hours. Just standing there in the cold. Takin' it."

"See," he continued. "We're workin', so we're warm. But you birders just stand there and take it."

"Boy," he said again. "You birders are tough."

"Darn right," I asserted, one man to another. "Takes one to know one," I added. "Nice jacket."

"Don't get to wear it much," he admitted.

Words to Lead By

To: An Incipient Field-trip Leader
From: The Bird Field-trip Support Force
RE: Your Request for Aid and Guidance

Dear Sir/Madam:

I am responding to your request for *"HELP!!!"* (emphasis yours) concerning the field trip you will shortly be leading for your local bird club. As you know, leading field trips is second only to writing collections of essays as a means of asserting your superior qualities within the birding community. However, convincing birders that you are more skilled and more knowledgeable than those you lead (particularly when this is not the case) can be challenging. Here are some helpful tips. Use them to advantage.

1. **Mumble.** Mumbling is a very useful technique. It helps keep the group cohesive (because everyone will be scrunching close trying to hear you), and it prevents people from contradicting you (you can't gainsay what you can't hear).
2. **Walk at the head of the line.** Always lead your group down narrow trails so patrons are forced to walk single file. Walking in front asserts your leadership status, and when birds are flushed you will be the only one to get a decent look at them.
3. **Never admit you are wrong.** Although correcting a misidentification may be helpful to incipient birders, it only serves to undermine your standing and that of fellow leaders. In the event of a boo-boo (e.g., a Ruby-crowned Kinglet inadvertently called

an Orange-crowned Warbler), it is best to quickly redirect the attention of the group to the "beautiful titmouse" nearby.

4. **Bring better binoculars.** Always wear the newest and most expensive roof-prism binoculars. They will intimidate people who are using binoculars that were not purchased by engaging the services of a mortgage company.

5. **Ditto for spotting scope.** Always invite other people to leave their scopes in the car (so that you can monopolize all long-distance identification). If a patron insists on bringing his or her scope, be certain you have a more powerful eyepiece and confide (loudly) that tests have shown that the performance of the other person's scope is undermined by severe chromatic aberrations. Sound apologetic.

6. **Name drop.** In casual conversation, mention your close association with birders whose names are well known and whose field abilities are genuine. Example 1: "When I pointed out to Jon (Dunn) that at temperatures over 86 degrees the tempo of a Kirtland's Warbler's tail wags increases by a factor . . . " Example 2: "Thank heavens David (Sibley) showed me the plates before the guide went to press. The embarrassment this error would have caused . . . "

7. **Avoid identification traps.** Bird identification is where the failings of most field-trip leaders are found out. Accordingly: never apply a name to a subject if you don't have to. Be subtle; be subjective. Suggest, don't divulge. Example 1: "First one of *those* today." Example 2: "Wow, good one!" Next, be current on all species splits and name changes (whether you can identify the bird or not). Not being able to find the names in the index of their field guides will keep followers so busy that they won't be able to bird. Then use Latin. Like you, most people will not admit when they don't know something. Using a bird's scientific name sounds impressive. If you don't know the names in Latin, make something up. Example 1: "Ah, *Empidonax enigma*! Note the bill extension." Example 2: "*Calidris beats-*

thehelloutofme for sure. See how small and brown it appears?" Finally, pin names to birds that are flying directly away or are cruising at altitudes that are barely suborbital; who's to say you are wrong? In the event that a bird doubles back and your Merlin is proven to be a Rock Dove, assert that you were looking at "the more distant bird." The one beyond the Rock Dove.

8. **Control bathroom stops.** Continue to promise a bathroom stop right up to the end of the trip. In case of a personal need, explain that you are leaving the group "to investigate a tantalizing chip note, alone, so that no one else will be subjected to [choose one or more] ticks / chiggers / scorpions / poison ivy / wolverines / land mines / carcinogenic contaminants."
9. **Always agree.** When someone asks whether such and such is a such and such, always say yes. Chances are that they are right, and if they aren't, they now have a vested interest in defending you against anyone who disagrees.
10. **All sparrows are Song Sparrows.**
11. **All hawks are Red-tailed Hawks.**
12. **Be vague on vocalizations.** Never get pinned down on a bird vocalization. All songs are "a little bit off." All calls are "not definitive." All unidentified vocalizations are titmice or jays.
13. **Avoid bird-rich areas.** When given a choice between an area that promises to hold birds and one devoid of them, choose the latter. Related to this, always bird into the sun (so birds will be reduced to silhouettes) and, wherever possible, approach roosting birds past their flush point so that looks will be fleeting and oblique.

Do not under any circumstances allow this letter to fall into the hands of patrons.

Good luck.

The Best Yard in the Neighborhood

This is a tribute to McDowell's Yard. When I was growing up, it was the uncontested best yard in the neighborhood.

No, it wasn't superbly landscaped. No, it never won the hotly contested title for "top lawn." What it did have was lots of heavily vegetated corners that didn't get much attention (another way of saying "were let go"). As a result, McDowell's Yard had more birds of more species than any of the properties tended by their *Home and Garden*–minded neighbors.

McDowell's Yard was the place where Red-winged Blackbirds returned first in the spring. This was because the whole back border was low and wet. Those cattail stalks left standing by winter winds became the flagpoles from which Red-wingeds ran up their colors in spring.

Similarly, McDowell's Yard was the haven for cardinals who passed up a whole neighborhood of well-trained hedges in favor of an unkempt tangle, and home to Field Sparrows who made their home in the unmowed expanse that did double duty as the neighborhood softball field.

And when that very first mockingbird showed up in the neighborhood back in 1960—should there have been any surprise that the rose tangle in McDowell's Yard seduced it to remain? From its perch, on the TV aerial of McDowell's house, it serenaded the neighborhood on moonlit nights, driving the cats to distraction and me to jealous envy.

Our yard (which never won top lawn honors, either) didn't boast the habitat and didn't have the birds. Robins, starlings, Blue

Jays, crows—all the indicator species of classically suburbanized yards. Only in one respect, and one area, did our yard best McDowell's—and that was in the migration category. In May, when oaks were in bloom, the woodland edge my parents left standing became a magnet for migrating songbirds. They made the branches animate and for a few short weeks made our yard the birding mecca of the neighborhood.

I didn't know anything about landscaping for nature back then—for that matter, neither did the McDowells. I didn't understand the cause-and-effect relationship between habitat and birds—didn't understand that the fruit-bearing trees found in McDowell's Yard (like wild cherry; like crabapple) were attractive to birds, and the ornamental trees that the rest of the neighborhood planted (like Japanese maple) were not. It was plain that hummingbirds and hummingbird moths preferred McDowell's flower garden to ours, but it didn't occur to me that the reason was the flowers.

All I knew (or cared about) was that when I wanted to see birds, McDowell's Yard was the place to go. It might never have won top lawn honors among the neighbors, but the birds, voting with their presence, called it best in show.

Crusader's Banner

I remember how I used to run, after the school bus dropped me off, before my life would be pressed into bondage by after-school chores. Down the trail through The Woods. Across the power line cut we called The Meadows. To the bulge of packed-clay shoreline know as The Beach of the Third (Brickyard) Pond. It wasn't far. Half a mile at most. Far enough to make my heart pump and cause jackets to be shed when the vantage of the beach was gained.

I came each evening for the show—whatever the season had to offer. That pond was the vessel from which seasons drew their strength; "The Beach" my private box seat. In March the dark leads of water that cut through the rotting ice spawned Ring-necked Ducks, the heralds of spring. In July, the trees hosted Scarlet Tanagers, Baltimore Orioles, and Red-eyed Vireos—the birds of youth and summer.

But in November, with winter sucking force from every shortening day, the ponds played a different drama on that revolving stage. Every evening, great flocks of Common Grackles would weave a path across the sky. Chin pressed to knees, I would watch, letting my imagination fly with them.

Sometimes I fancied the flocks a defeated army, strung out like Napoleon's troops as they retreated from Russia. Sometimes, I likened them to autumn's banner, held aloft by great, invisible hands, rising and falling defiantly in the shallow November light.

Sometimes, as the light grew thin, as the sky went from blue to violet and from violet to red, I was brought to recall the Children's Crusade—the flight of faith that led only to bondage.

Most of the time, I simply watched. The massed spectacle of birds moving in empathetic accord. Heralding from who knew where. Bound for what, I couldn't say.

What bound me to them was the journey itself. It seemed like life—an umbilical cord made up of little things that knit the beginning to the end, horizon to horizon. It seemed, when you focused upon individual birds, too ordinary to care about. But when you regarded the entirety of the flock, reaching beyond the opposing horizons, it was too great to contemplate.

I'm not going to tell you that I really, consciously, thought these things at the age of ten. I can only tell you that I felt them—and still do. Every time I see those flocks of black birds rising and falling across an autumn sky.

I know that grackles are not universally esteemed. I know they predate upon the nests and young of many woodland species and that they keep smaller birds from the feeder. I don't turn a blind eye to their golden eye, and I try not to be seduced by the iridescent magic locked in their feathers.

My loyalty to them is tempered, like the message that they as autumn's heralds bring. That all things are transitory. That maybe it is passage, not objective, that defines our lives. That some day, when the last winds of autumn fail and the last banner falls, the journey will end.

Only the stage will remain.

Donna and the Right Stuff

This one's for Donna. Donna McDowell, my old birding chum. The one who got me birding. This isn't her name, now. Donna's married, moved, living in . . . Well, I can't say.

Fact is, I haven't seen Donna in over thirty adult years. But back when time was measured in the number of days you could get out of a pair of jeans, and the world's two superpowers were making their first tentative probes of space, Washington Avenue's two, young superbirders were exploring the forgotten world called Whippany, New Jersey.

In our hands were two catalytic tools—as critical to our efforts to understand the world around us as a booster rocket is to getting Sputniks in space. These were: binoculars and a field guide. Two presents given to honor a birthday. They changed our world. While all the adults were looking up at little things that went blink in the night, we were looking up . . . and down—at tree sparrows whose caps were red and whose calls were as brittle as winter ice, at juncos who disappeared with a twittering and a bracketing flash of white.

At Rose-breasted Grosbeaks! Probably the most beautiful bird in the world (maybe even the universe)! It was Donna who dared and double-dared me to shinny up a nearby tree and see how many downy young were in the nest. It was Donna who led the delegation of two to the home owner's door to impress upon him the significance of having the most beautiful bird in the universe in his yard.

He *was* impressed. Impressed that while the other kids in the neighborhood were seeking diversion, we were seeking discoveries—and finding them, unlooked for, in suburban backyards. We could do this because we had the right stuff—binoculars around our necks and a bird book in our pockets.

Other kids dreamed of being astronauts—and some of them succeeded. Many kids had no dreams at all and, maybe because of this, grew up and became adults.

But Donna and I didn't have to realize our dream. We lived it. Every day. In the woods and fields and tree-rimmed backyards that defined the orbit of our existence. Because discovery, like the universe, began at our own back doors. And because we had the right stuff.

Of Kids and Model Airplanes

We, meaning the board of directors of a national birding organization, were meeting in some airport hotel. The subject was youth and birding. Why more young people were not involved. How the future of birding was dependent upon early recruitment. How wayward young adults might be spared lives of indolence, violence, somnambulation, and computer-joystick-related injuries if only they would discover what we had discovered: the joy of birding.

We were pretty serious about this topic (as adults tend to be). Our discussion had exhausted the recruitment potential of young birder clubs/camps/outings/newsletters and Web sites. We'd moved on to mentors programs and essay contests. But having crossed a critical threshold in coffee ingestion/ expulsion, I excused myself and carried the topic with me into the men's lavatory. There was one guy there ahead of me. As is my perpetual fortune, the guy was a talker.

"You're from that bird-watching group, right?" he said.

"Uh-huh," I said.

"I'm with the (choose one)—American, North American, International, Intergalactic—Association of Model Airplane (choose one)—Builders, Designers, Flyers, Collectors." Sorry I can't be more specific. I was deep in thought.

"We're having our annual meeting," he continued.

"Terrific," I said.

"Model airplanes is a great hobby," he added.

"I'll bet," I replied, concluding that this guy and I could have nothing in common. But I was wrong.

"We're discussing ways of getting more young people involved in model airplanes," he said. "You know, it's important for young people to find wholesome activities, and unless more kids get interested in flying model airplanes, this hobby is just going to . . . "

I walked away refreshed—on more counts than one—and found myself a good deal more relaxed about the youth/birding problem.

Don't get me wrong. I'm not saying that kids shouldn't be encouraged to go birding. I'm also not saying that there shouldn't be a social and information network that caters to young birders. I'm just saying this. When *I* was a kid, if some well-intentioned adult wearing a big, sincere, adult grin had said: "Pete, you should go bird watching because it's fun and will help make you a better person," the suggestion would automatically have claimed first place on my short list of LAST THING I WILL EVER DO.

Maybe times have changed, but when I was a kid, adults ran everything—including my life. School, chores, meals, TV time, everything. But there was one thing the adults didn't control. That was birding.

So when I got home from school, I ran in the front door, grabbed my binoculars, and ran out the back door into the woods before any adults could further mess up my life.

In plain, honest fact, one of the primary reasons I went birding was to get *away* from adults. So I have a suggestion. A strategy to be used by adults who are worried about the future of birding and want very much to get young people involved.

Give a kid binoculars and a bird book. Walk away.

Don't organize anything. Don't sweat the details. Just give a kid the catalytic tools they need to engage birds. Then be a good catalyst and disappear.

Binoculars and a field guide. One confers supernatural intimacy. The other unlocks the secrets of each bird's identity. You've got flint; you've got steel. The natural inquisitiveness of children is tinder.

The only other ingredient needed to kindle a flame is air,

space, the freedom to let young minds engage birds on their own terms, in their own fashion, at a level that excites and invites them. I have a lot of faith in the capacity of birds to captivate and a lot of childhood memories to support this.

Don't worry that eager young birders are not flocking to your monthly meetings. Remember, they don't drive and they don't have the scheduling latitude of adults.

Don't worry because the majority of teens seem dispassionate about going on the Saturday morning bird walk. There are passions and there are passions. You may have forgotten this, but trust people in their teens to know where the accent in passion goes.

And while we're discussing bird clubs and demographics, organizations probably shouldn't worry overmuch about the disproportionately small representation of young adults in the ranks, either. Developing careers, finding a partner, parenting, and paying for it all is pretty all-consuming.

Have a little faith. Have a little patience. Have a long-term recruitment strategy that begins with giving a kid a pair of binoculars, a bird book, and a bond to call his or her own. Someday, after kids are raised and the career ladder has been climbed, that one-time young birder will remember how much fun they used to have finding birds. And wonder, maybe . . .

Whether there aren't any organizations for bird watching. Like that organization for people who fly model airplanes. The National, International, Intergalactic Something or Other that that old guy I met in the men's room was talking about the other day . . .

Going to the Bird Store. Hoping for a Guide

It wasn't until I started laying out my equipment in the airport rental car that I realized I'd left my field guide at home. Thinking quickly (because I was wasting valuable birding time), I went to the nearest phone booth, leafed through the white pages, and found a listing under "B" for "Birds, Birds, Birds."

"Everything," the boxed ad promised, "for the bird enthusiast." It was only five minutes away.

"Can I help you?" a cherubic young lad asked from behind the counter.

"Yes," I said, "I'd like to buy a field guide."

"A what?" he replied.

"A field guide?" I repeated.

"A person?" he asked.

"A book," I said to uncomprehending eyes. "A field guide to birds," I explained, fully expecting to see the spark of understanding. I was wrong.

"Never heard of it," he said.

"Not 'it.' Them," I explained. "There are dozens of field guides on the market."

"OK," he said. "I never heard of *them*. What do you use them for?"

"THEY HELP IDENTIFY THE BIRDS YOU SEE, YOU DOLT." I shouted. Looking around the store. Assuming I'd find a bookshelf that I could point to. Discovering I was wrong.

"Huh," he said. "Never seen anything like that. Are you sure you're in the right place?"

"This is a store that caters to people who like birds, right?"

"Right."

"But you don't sell field guides?"

"Nope."

I walked outside to make certain the planet I was on was indeed orbiting around a single, yellow sun, then I went back inside.

"Can I see the manager?" I asked.

"Field guide," she said, savoring the term. Favoring me with a smile. "Maybe if you explain to me what it's used for."

"It helps you identify the birds you see," I said.

"Identifies them as birds?" she asked.

"Identifies them to species."

"Oh," she said. "We don't have anything like that."

"This is a bird store," I asserted.

"This is a bird store," she affirmed.

"But you don't sell field guides."

"We don't sell field guides."

"What do you sell?" I asked, somewhat perplexed.

"Everything to do with birds," she said with a sweep of her hand. "Decorative plates of birds. Coaster sets with birds. Bird lawn ornaments. Bird door knockers. Bird lamp shades. Bird playing cards. Bird calendars. Bird stationery. Everything for the person who loves birds."

"But nothing that helps you identify them?"

"They have feathers," she explained.

"I know they have feathers," I affirmed.

"That's how you know they are birds," she replied, brusquely.

"I could have told him *that*," the young clerk chimed.

"Shut up," I observed. "Look," I said to the owner, "I'm a birder who is visiting the area for the first time. I am not familiar with many of the species you have here. I'm looking for *something* that will help me put names to the birds I see."

"Oh," she chirped. "I have something that might work." She walked toward a display and picked up a dishtowel boasting an assortment of British finches and birds of paradise.

"The names are printed right next to them," she noted.

"Does it come in any color but yellow?"

"Egg yolk," she corrected. "No, it doesn't."

"I don't think so," I said.

"It's on sale," she confided.

"It's not what I want," I responded. "And I'd look pretty ridiculous walking around High Island with a dish towel in my back pocket. What I need is a bird book."

"A bird book!" she exclaimed, walking toward another display and handing me a coffee table-sized tome entitled *Bird Masterpieces*. In it was a collection of the world's most famous paintings with birds dubbed in. Birds sitting around conversing at the Last Supper . . . birds melting off tables . . . "The Mona Limpkin" . . .

"No field guides," I said, beginning to grasp the obvious.

"No field guides," she agreed.

"Because this is a *bird* store," I said.

"Yes. This is a *bird* store," she confirmed.

"I see. Well, can you think of anyplace that might sell me a book like the one I described?"

"You might try a garden center," she suggested. "They sell bird feeders and birdhouses there."

"Or the grocery store," the young employee added. "They have a book section."

"Thank you," I said. "I'll try them. Say, you wouldn't happen to have a universal rain guard in stock, would you?"

"A what?" they said in unison.

"A rain guard for my binoculars?"

"This is a bird store," they reminded me.

"Oh, right," I said.

What was I thinking?

The Take-Home of Going Away

We dropped the luggage on the floor and looked around. Not surprisingly, the house had not changed since we'd locked the door, pocketed the key, and gone off on our adventure.

Linda, the practical one, started putting groceries away. I stepped outside. After seven weeks in places like the Galapagos, the Andes, the Amazon Basin, Chile, Tierra del Fuego, the Antarctic, and the Falklands, home was going to take some getting used to.

So, I assumed, were the everyday birds of our yard.

Over the course of our travels, we'd seen many of the planets most-celebrated birds. Andean Condors that flew like Icarus. Cock-of-the-Rocks whose sunrise-colored raiment is to splendor what a symphony is to sound. Tanagers of every stripe and hue, hummingbirds whose plumages humbled rainbows, and butterflies whose kaleidoscopic wings humbled them. Giant Petrels and Little Shearwaters. Mockingbirds so tame that they mistook us for perches, and the finches that gave Darwin the key that unlocked in his mind the mechanics of creation.

Next to all of this splendor, the birds of my backyard were going to seem pretty ordinary (or so I thought).

But I was wrong.

Sitting on the bottom perch of the thistle feeder, clad in winter drab, was a single goldfinch. The bird was very preoccupied, untroubled by my approach. She let me to within a dozen feet, and when I raised my binoculars and trained them upon her, I could see my reflection poised in the portal of her eye.

In her eye I could see the same figure reflected that I'd seen just a few days earlier in the eye of a nesting Wandering Albatross.

In her eye I could see the alert intensity of a bird going about the business of being a bird (as birds the world over do).

In her eye I could see the same flame of life that had burned in the azure-colored eye of a Flightless Cormorant in the Galapagos, the somber eye of a Wandering Albatross on South Georgia, the amber-shrouded eye of a Chinstrap Penguin on the Antarctic Peninsula.

In her eye I could see everything. All the genetic possibilities that were ever realized, all the possibilities that ever yet may be. All that may be seen in the eye of any bird anywhere on this planet, and this:

That all the pleasure and wonder and fun of birds are to be found as much in a suburban backyard as at the farthest reaches of the planet.

That was the take-home of going away.

Want to Go for a Walk?

Can I ask you a question?

Thank you. I'll make this quick.

Do you like birds?

Stupid question. Of course you like birds. Most people do. You like to watch them because they are entertaining. You like to hear them because they complement the world with their song.

So why is it that you've never gone on an organized bird walk?

BIRD WALK, n. An organized (maybe semiorganized) field trip, orchestrated by a bird-oriented organization or institution, that leads directly to the world of birds. Millions of people have made this avocational leap. It has changed their lives.

I know. I know. Stop. What you are telling me is that what you really love are the birds in your yard.

Absolutely! They're like family. You know them; they know you. They don't hide when you approach (like other birds). They don't live in buggy places. You don't even have to go out of the way to see them (because they share your corner of the world).

All these things are so.

Let me ask you another question.

Do you like to eat?

Sure you do. And while there is nothing better than a home-cooked meal, I'll bet you enjoy dining out now and again, going to restaurants that specialize in cuisine that caters to your more exotic tastes or features entrées that are too much trouble to make at home.

Well, going on a bird trip is a little like going out to dinner. It doesn't replace your kitchen; it just adds another pleasurable dimension to your experience.

It doesn't matter if you've never gone on a field trip before. Going on a field trip isn't like stepping onto a dance floor. All you have to do is amble along with the group. Let somebody else lead.

It doesn't matter if you don't show up wearing the hottest new binoculars or a spotting scope that looks like it was designed by a NASA engineer. In fact, it probably doesn't matter if you don't have binoculars that are working at (or near) par. Most people who lead field trips pack an extra pair or two (just in case).

Do it! Check the outdoors column in your local newspaper (bird clubs and nature centers as well as local and county parks often list their trip schedules there). Visit a store in your area that specializes in birdseed or products. They may offer walks themselves. If not, they will almost certainly be in contact with those institutions that do.

Do it! Go on a bird walk. You'll get to know a whole new set of birds—probably acquaintances of the birds you call family. It will open your eyes to ways of seeing and appreciating birds you never dreamed of. It will put you in contact with people who share your interest and will plant your feet on an avenue of wonder and discovery.

I saved the best for last. Many bird walks, perhaps most, are also free. Search high and low, this side of your fence or the other; you'll not find a better deal than free.

Birding in Shadowland

I enjoy birding by myself. One on one. Just me and whatever the northwest winds ferry my way. But while I may go unaccompanied, in Cape May, New Jersey, and elsewhere, I am never so arrogant as to think that I bird alone. Every step I take falls in the footsteps of birders who came before. Every time I raise binoculars, there are two sets of hands bringing the instruments to bear—one flesh and blood, one woven of the shadows cast by those ornithological giants who came before and whose knowledge is my hereditary foundation.

Perhaps more than any other birding hotspot, Cape May is a land where spirits abound. Many bird students whose names are spoken in awe and reverence left their indelible mark on the peninsula.

First and foremost is Alexander Wilson who, along with his companion George Ord, made six trips to the Cape. It was here, while searching for the birds that were to occupy the pages of Wilson's *American Ornithology*, that the pair collected the plover that bears Wilson's name and the warbler whose name continues to honor the peninsula today.

No less illustrious was John James Audubon, the pioneer bird illustrator. The author of *Birds of America* spent a summer collecting and painting in the marshes of Great Egg Harbor. Spencer Baird (of sparrow and sandpiper fame) made repeated trips to the Cape, although it must be said that his interest in the region was not purely ornithological. Both he and his brother William married sisters who lived in the town of Cape May Court House, the county seat.

Witmer Stone, of the Philadelphia Academy of Science, codified his regional affinity in his two-volume treatise, *Bird Studies at Old Cape May*. And in 1934, the year his famous field guide was published, Roger Tory Peterson joined a young warden named Robert P. Allen to conduct the first, full-season hawk count in Cape May.

This is just a short list of some giants of the past, the ones whose shadows fall across mine and whose pooled knowledge courses along my synaptic circuitry. There are other giants to be sure. Living giants like David Sibley, Paul Lehman, Clay Sutton, Michael O'Brien—birders whose shadows have not yet reached their living potential, birders whose skills overshadow even the efforts of our ancestors.

But the reason that this is so, the reason that the reach of their skills is greater, is that these giants of the present stand on the shoulders of those who came before. The shadows they cast don't cross, but merge.

So when I go birding, in Cape May and elsewhere, I never go alone. Like a thrush moving beneath the canopy, like a hawk watcher whose raised hand shields his eyes, my efforts are aided by a cast of shadows. While reaching for the stars, as every generation does, I stand in the cool confidence of the shade.

Stuff E'nuf?

When I was seven, I owned a pair of 6x binoculars and a bird book that fit into a hip pocket with room to spare. I'd get home from school. Shed slacks. Don jeans. Grab bins. Pocket the book. Sprint out the back door and start looking at birds.

It was a blast.

I have just finished packing for a trip to Arizona and I darn near had a nervous breakdown sorting through all the bird-finding stuff I've accumulated, trying to decide . . . Should I pack the 10x binoculars to cut the distance on those wide-open western spaces, or a close-focusing 7x for birding in those canyon confines?

I opted for the ten. Changed my mind and selected the seven. Reconsidered and switched to a good, versatile 8x instead. Then I threw the seven in, too (in case my primary glass went down and I needed a backup).

Why not the 10x? Because, I reasoned, a spotting scope would provide extra magnification when I needed it—but which scope? The 60mm was more compact and a better traveler, but the 78mm was a better performer. If I chose the 78, it would be prudent to bring the 20-60x zoom eyepiece because the fixed 30x eyepiece becomes a functional 38x when mated to the larger objective, and this would mean having to bring the larger, more stable tripod instead of the one that fit in my travel bag.

Of course, this would mean having to include a scope-carrying pack because the magnum scope/mega tripod package is too heavy to sling over your shoulder and tote all day.

I re-reconsidered just bringing the 10x binoculars and forgetting the scope but ended up taking the mega/magnum scope package *and* the 10x binoculars (reasoning that if the scope got too heavy I could leave it in the car and fall back on the bins).

Oh, yeah, I packed the zoom eyepiece, too.

"It's small," I concluded.

After great debate, I chose only two regional bird-finding guides from my library; two general field guides (one had better hummingbird illustrations; the other was better on flycatchers); specialty guides for hawks, warblers, and sparrows; and, after a short debate, Peter Grant's *Gulls*.

"Gulls wander," I reasoned. "You just never know."

I felt so good about keeping my arsenal of books so trim that I splurged and threw in *two* field guides to the birds of Mexico, two guides specializing in separation of closely allied species, and guides to wildflowers, butterflies, geology, herps, mammals, insects, and meteorology.

After a short internal debate, I pulled the meteorology book and packed a weather-band radio instead.

"Let the experts do their job," I concluded.

Of course, clothing represented a challenge. All those elevation changes, all those temperature swings. Being a veteran traveler, I used the old layer system—packed everything I owned in layers, starting with the heavy wool stuff at the bottom of the bag, and leaving the light, lofty, techweenie stuff for the top.

I limited myself to one pair of light hiking boots, two pairs of running shoes, wellies, and two rain parka/pants combinations (in case one got wet).

"Just no accounting for that El Niño," I reasoned.

Incidentals included two bird-vocalization cassette sets (one had better variety, the other better nocturnals), a 100,000-candlepower flashlight, two water bottles, and a portable planetarium. Then I packed the camping gear. I planned on staying out one night . . . maybe two.

So, after everything that was defensibly essential was packed, and everything that was indefensibly expendable expended, I was left with more birding-related stuff than Columbus could have carted in three ships bound for the New World.

What I want to know is: When am I going to have enough stuff to enjoy birding as much as I did when I was seven years old and just ran into the woods with a pair of 6x binoculars?

Which kind of makes you wonder why nobody is marketing a good 6x glass anymore. Boy, I'd love to have one of those babies for backyard birding or dense woodlands where depth of field becomes a serious concern and . . .

A Six-Pack of Fame

"I know you," the liquor-store owner shouted from across the counter (and a distance of three feet).

"Yeah, I'm a patron," I said, wishing it weren't so. It wasn't the kind of liquor store in which you might buy a fine Merlot to impress friends. It was the kind in which you might buy lottery tickets, beer, and jug wine for the times you aren't impressing friends.

"I mean you're that bird-watching guy, right? The one on the CD-ROM. Hey!" he shouted to several wrestling fans stocking up on brews for the Monday night bloodfest, "This guy's a famous bird watcher."

Never has anonymity seemed so dear.

Don't get me wrong. I'm vain. I like recognition. But writers are usually better known than recognized. I'm more used to dealing with people who only assume they know me, as opposed to people who actually do.

Take the guy I ran into at the Cape May Hawk Watch one day, one of those name-dropper types. Faster than you can say "Hi, how are you?", he struck up a conversation focused upon his favorite theme.

"Hey, do you know Harold Axtell?" he invited. I assured him I did.

"Me and Harold bird together all the time. Do you know Roger Tory Peterson?"

I told him we'd met, and learned, predictably, that he and Roger birded together all the time, too.

"Do you know Pete Dunne?"

I considered saying "no" because I've made the study of this individual my life's work and I cannot honestly say that I have reached my ambition—but "yes" seemed closer to the truth. Much to my surprise, I learned that this gentleman and I went birding together all the time, too!

At this point someone on the platform pointed out that I was Pete Dunne. Hesitating only a moment, the man introduced himself and suggested we go birding.

On several occasions I've had people come up to me and start reminiscing about the time we birded Big Bend or Gambell or some other place I've never been. When I point this out, they seem momentarily perplexed, and then ask: "Aren't you Kenn Kaufman?"

"No," I'll reply. "Kenn's a better birder than I am. I'm the writer who birds; Kenn's the birder who writes."

"Oh," they'll say.

There was another, wonderfully sublime occasion when I was to keynote an assembly of wildlife educators at their annual conference. The person who introduced me, the director of a state fish and game department, whipped the audience into a frenzy of anticipation by expounding upon exploits that included years of leading tours, acknowledged expertise in the field of bird identification, and authorship of one of birding's most celebrated field guides.

I was mentally preparing to open my address with a humble disclaimer—but that proved unnecessary.

"Ladies and Gentlemen," she said, "Please welcome Jon Dunn."

Oh, well. Jon's a better birder, too.

You can't spend twenty-five years in a field and remain anonymous forever. Every printed mug shot is a nail in anonymity's coffin. Every appearance on the banquet circuit is a coming-out. Still, I wasn't prepared for celebrity status in the local package-goods store.

"No kidding," one of the several beefy patrons intoned, walking over, reaching out to take my hand. "What's it like being a famous bird watcher?" he asked.

"Pretty ordinary . . . in an unconventional way."

"My wife likes birds," he continued.

"Small world," I said. "Can I have my change, please?"

"Hey, do you know that guy who works at that bird place in Cape May?"

"Jon Kaufman."

"Yeah, that's the guy. I read somethin' about him doin' this twenty-four-hour bird-watching contest. Hey, you want a beer?"

Fame.

Explorers (of the Lost World) Club

Office of the Surviving Cocaptain

Dear Initiate,

Just recently, several minutes ago in fact, a vote was taken and a decision made to open the rolls of the Explorers Club to potential new members. I nominated you.

You should know that this moment has no precedents—not in the forty-three-year history of this prestigious organization. You should also know that insofar as all club officers were not present, the decision was made by a quorum of half—this being myself. Donna Jean McDowell, childhood chum, cocaptain, cofounder (and only other member) could not be reached and may not, in point of fact, have maintained her membership.

There are, after all, many obstacles that may fall between a person and childhood (among them maturation, mate selection, marriage, mortgages, PTA meetings, college-tuition payments, taxes, and taxes' twin affliction—death). Donna may, or may not, recall the pioneering achievements that mark the illustrious history of the Explorers—a legacy which includes the discovery and subsequent exploration of wonders like Dry Swamp, Big-X Swamp, and [Old Man] Kordock's [Field].

These places were once as uncharted as darkest Africa, or the North Pole. But unlike these celebrated regions, you won't find the names Big-X or Kordock's Field on any commercially published maps. No map showing their location survived the sack of childhood.

Also, and sad to relate, you will not find Dry Swamp, Big-X Swamp, or Kordock's in physical fact—even if your exploring skills are as polished as Donna's and mine were when we explored the world with seven- and nine-year-old eyes. These locations surrendered long ago to human ambitions that ran counter to the right of special places to exist—which, incidentally, is why you have been nominated to membership in the club.

I am mortally afraid that these childhood haunts survive only in the mind of what may be the only recalling member of the old Explorers Club. The loss of these memories would make the loss complete. If you accept membership in the club, and if anything should happen to me, it is your duty to keep their memory and significance alive.

I tell you plainly that there was no place in all of Whippany, New Jersey, better suited for finding Spotted Turtles than Dry Swamp—before it was named and before it was dry (which is to say, before the guys from the county mosquito commission arrived with their backhoe). After very wet springs, the swamp would regain some of its aquatic properties, and the place, for a short time, would become amphibian-rich again. In winter, there was sometimes enough ice in isolated pools to serve as a skating rink—providing you didn't mind sharing the surface with a plentitude of tussock grass hummocks.

But the turtles went with the standing water in the summer of 1957, and many wonderful turtle-catching years that would have followed were denied.

Happily the guys with the backhoe missed Big-X Swamp. It was too overgrown to be found by a grown-up, and the old drainage ditch that they connected to the newly built one was easily dammed.

Big-X was a mosaic of red maple, tussock grass, and pools that could soak you to the knees if your sneakers failed to bond with a particularly treacherous tussock. It would hold water all summer in all but the driest years. The waters were home to all manner of Green Frogs, bullfrogs, and leopard frogs whose sole purpose in life seemed to be waiting to be caught by hand.

But once, in that aquatic tangle, a pair of Wood Duck landed.

The male was so beautiful that it made a person ache worse than you'd ache from eating ice cream too fast, and when the birds flushed, the female's squeal caused goose bumps.

The swamp's integrity remained intact until it was filled to serve as a parking lot for a trucking company some years after the Explorers Club disbanded (and before club members reached an age at which the significance of habitat loss might be fully appreciated). Now, this place too exists only in memory.

Memory for memory, no place is more anchored than Kordock's Field. This grassy expanse, kept open by one stubborn old hermit's scythe-wielding hand, was rich in living things. Principle among them were Red-winged Blackbirds that hovered like dragonflies and "kack . . . kack . . . kacked" like Geiger counters. The closer you got to the bird's nest, the faster and louder it kacked.

I will forever attribute my familiarity with the sparrow-like female Red-winged Blackbird to those many in-your-face encounters. But the discovery that earned Kordock's an inviolate corner of my mind had to do with a warbler. A black-masked wraith called Maryland Yellowthroat. It was there, in Kordock's Field, in the summer I became a bird watcher, that I found a yellowthroat nest! To this day, the only Maryland (even Common) Yellowthroat nest I have ever seen.

It was tiny, tightly woven, and tucked in a tussock. It was perfect and round, and the vessel for three perfect eggs. It lives in my mind almost as vividly as it lived the summer it existed in fact. So you see how important it is that you make room in your mind for this memory, too.

The people who live in the homes that were built on the site after Old Man Kordock died know nothing of yellowthroats or nests or their significance. They may be innocent, but, as evidenced by the lawns that spread a green shroud over the habitat that was, they are also ignorant (and therefore not eligible for membership in the club).

And see. I have drawn you a map. Drawn it from a memory that seems to fasten more easily to events that engaged my mind thirty years ago than to those of thirty minutes ago. In this respect, it is not drawn to scale.

Only tested and card-carrying members of the Explorers Club are allowed to see it. Because need supersedes procedure, I am waiving the customary initiation. You will not have to have all ten fingers pricked with a real sharp thorn. You will not have to shinny to the top of a twenty-foot maple and ride it, Robert Frost–style, to the ground. You will not even have to identify twenty birds without using "the book."

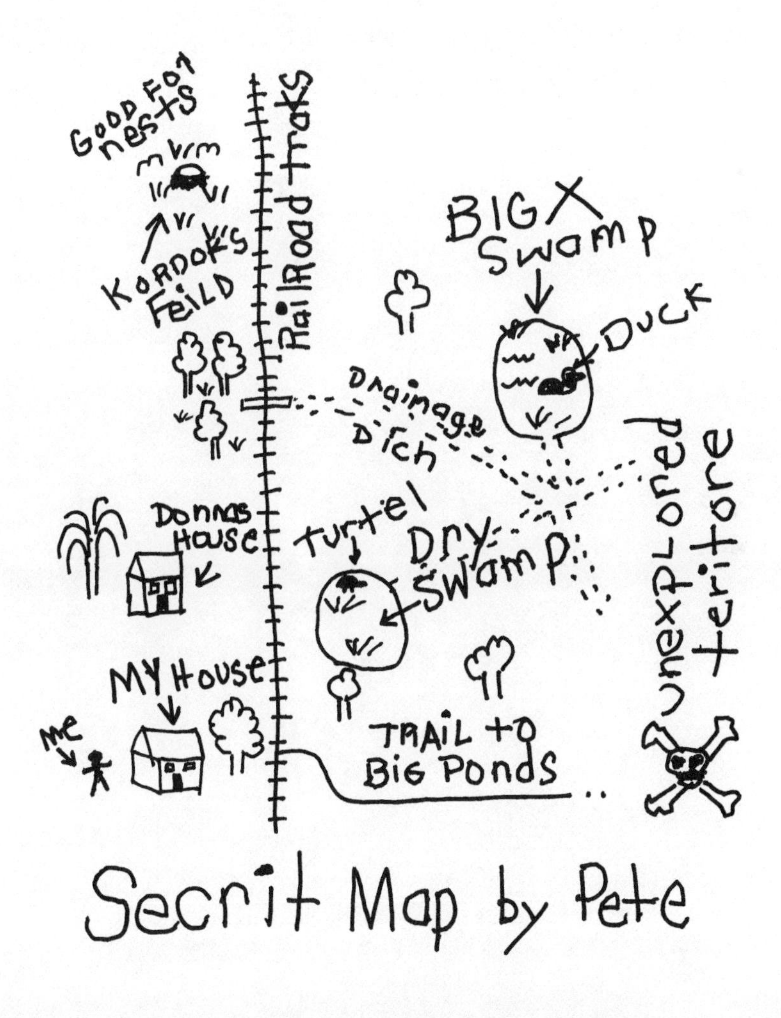

All you have to do is chant: "Dry Swamp, Big-X Swamp, and Kordock's Field." This and your resolve to keep small, natural pockets within the exploring reach of children is all that is required of an Explorer.

Welcome to the club.

Sincerely,
Pete Dunne, Cocaptain, The Explorers

P.S. If you meet Donna, her code name is "Oriole."
P.P.S. I'll teach you the secret yodel another time.
P.P.P.S. Don't let this map fall into enemy hands.

Earl's Journal

This one's for Earl. The man who introduced me to the most important book I own. It isn't a field guide. It isn't a collection of finely wrought essays. What it is is a dog-eared journal, and it records the natural events that have intersected my life.

Earl kept such a journal. His example, as well as his approach to the natural world, left their mark upon me.

Earl was a farmer. He lived in Ohio. He raised corn and cattle and gladioli. He was also a keen observer of nature. Someone who thought of a bird as more than a check mark in a book. Someone who wanted to know more about the Carolina Wrens that nested in the old couch in the shed than just how to tell them from Bewick's Wren.

He led a hard life and went about his chores with the devotion of a man born to the plow, but a part of Earl's mind was always on the world around him. What he discovered, he recorded each evening in his journal.

When the first frost sparkled on the grass, the milestone was duly noted. The morning in March when the phoebes arrived was worth an entry—and got one in 1946 . . . and 1947 . . . and 1957 and 1967, too.

If a Cooper's Hawk killed a junco. If the Red-tailed Hawks changed nest sites. If the fireflies were particularly numerous. If the Buckeyes were scant. If a comet crossed the sky—all these things were recorded. Because they were significant enough to note, and because Earl imbued them with significance.

Who knows what is cause and what is effect? All I know is

that, as a nine-year-old budding naturalist, I marveled at the storehouse of events recorded in the pages of Earl's journal and vowed that someday I'd have an entry-rich journal, too.

Comets don't cross the sky every day. Great, journal-worthy events seemed hard to come by at first. So I was forced to look hard and close and long at everyday things to fill those pages. And you know what? The closer I looked, the more journal-worthy entries I found.

Take Carolina Wrens! As documented in the pages of my journal, they sing every month of the year. Take Carolina Wren nests. Did you know that the birds use paper and snake skins and string and feathers in the construction?

A birder may overlook these things, but not a bird *watcher* and certainly not a bird watcher who keeps a journal—the most important book I own.

So here's to you, Earl. Thank you for giving me the discipline to look close. Like you, I now have a storehouse of events logged in ledgers. The encounters are mine. The credit, yours.

A Flicker Day for Sure

I was heading up the drive to New Jersey Audubon's Scherman Hoffman Sanctuary. The trees were touched with autumn, and the branches were bowing to the wind. Along the drive, big-bodied birds exploded into motion as the car passed. The migrant woodpeckers flashed yellow underwings and displayed telltale white rumps.

"Going to be a flicker day on the phone," I knew even before I parked my car. When you spend as much time as I have in the old natural history racket, these insights come easily.

I don't know what it is about nature that paralyzes home owners. Maybe it's cultural estrangement, maybe it's this age's reverence for the "expert opinion," but every time somebody's suburban tranquility is shattered by an encounter with Ma Nature, they run to the phone and call *the nature center naturalist!* In this age of this world, *these* are the arbitrators in man vs. nature conflicts.

The ones who tell the painters how long it takes House Finches to hatch and fledge.

"Sorry, guys. Maybe you can come back and do the porch in October."

The ones who can talk a fist full of baby robin out of a possessive six-year-old's grasp, convince a ninety-two-year-old park patron to stop throwing white bread to the ducks, and listen to a caller's description of a bird that is . . .

"Orange and white and big as a crow with a sharp beak and long legs, no tail, and circles all around its face . . . "

. . . and *still* come up with the correct identification of "Killdeer."

Put your average naturalist in a sensory deprivation chamber, leave them stranded for six months, then plug them into a nature-center phone line, and they will be able to tell you the date (with a week's variance) in three calls or fewer.

Here in New Jersey, the crisis-call calendar begins in February with the onset of the old kamikaze-cardinal-throwing-itself-against-the-window call.

"No, ma'am, the bird is not trying to break into your child's bedroom. It's just seeing its reflection in the window and defending its territory from a perceived rival."

In March it proceeds to woodpeckers that drum a morning tattoo on drainpipes, House Finches that fuse screen doors shut with their nests in April, and domestic-minded Barn Swallows that undermine the aesthetic integrity of garage-parked cars in May, before moving on to the seasonal flood of "BBCs" (baby-bird calls) that command the summer months.

And then comes October, and in suburban neighborhoods all across America, residents wake up, look outside, and see this strange bird . . .

"It's all brown with black spots," they explain. "It has a red patch on the back of its head. A great big black V on its chest. It can't walk and it's been sitting on our lawn all morning and . . . "

Not all the callers that nature centers entertain are cordial. I recall one irate coastal home owner, living near to the Stone Harbor heron rookery, who was incensed that a big white bird was standing in his driveway. "As a taxpayer," he demanded that I come and remove the bird.

My elaborate reply involved the essence of free will, an exploration of Great Egret fledgling behavior, and a lecture on the importance of self-reliance and self-determination in American culture.

He still insisted that I come and remove the bird.

I went on to explain the subtle difference between tax-supported government agencies and tax-exempt research and education facilities, at which point the caller screamed that he was going to punch me in the face and hung up.

Honesty compels me to admit that not all the responses nature centers make to pleas for assistance are cordial, either. I recall one harried director of a coastal research center who impetuously and inopportunely answered the phone one day. After five minutes of not being able to get a word in edgewise, then learning that the injured bird compromising his schedule was *"a blasted pigeon,"* the director (who was, oh-by-the-way, a marine biologist, not a birder) suggested that the caller "step on its head."

The center's funding, needless to say, was heavily endowed, *not* dependent upon gifts and contributions.

While I understand the time constraints of busy center directors, I have always tried to be cordial to crisis callers even when I could not be helpful. But I have demands upon my time, too, and deadlines to meet. When I get to work at 7:30 A.M., it means that my docket is clogged. Calls that come in before regular work hours, are dispatched, whenever possible, with alacrity.

Sure enough, the phone was ringing when I put my key in the door. It continued to ring as I went into the kitchen and started making coffee. It stopped . . . then started again as I moved for my office. I picked it up on the fifth ring.

"It's a flicker," I chanted into the mouthpiece.

"What?" a somewhat startled voice inquired.

"It's a flicker," I repeated, in my most cheerful voice.

There was a moment's stunned silence, then a cautious inquiry. "Is this the Audubon Society?"

"Yes, ma'am," I replied.

"Oh, good. Maybe you can help me. There's this strange bird sitting on our lawn that's all brown with black spots and . . ."

No doubt about it. A flicker day for sure.

The Errors We're Known By

Somewhere along the line, I became known as a great birder. The kind of birder who can look at an Empidonax flycatcher and describe it down to the submolecular level, someone who can study a stint and tell you which side of the nest it fledged from.

While it's wonderful to be thought of as a great birder, it is however, in my case, not true. To paraphrase and apply a favorite old nursery rhyme to my abilities: when I am good, I am middle-average good; but when I am bad, I am horrid.

Horrid! Take, for example, the time I picked out a female diving duck on some lake in Minnesota. Had the lake been one of those lonely North Woods lakes, everything would have been fine. Unfortunately, this was a very public lake, one being popularized by about 400 American Birding Association Conference–goers.

The duck (which was, I feel compelled to point out in my own defense, pretty distant) looked like a scaup. My rule for distinguishing Greater and Lesser Scaup is a simple one. If the head suggests Ring-necked Duck, it's Lesser. This bird's head did indeed suggest Ring-necked Duck, and there was a reason for this, a reason that 400 members of the ABA very gleefully pointed out to me at the species tally.

It *was* a Ring-necked Duck.

Take, for example, the "Red-tailed Hawk" that I pointed out to the members of my Raptor Identification Workshop one September afternoon. "White underparts, bold patterning on the wings, reddish tail," I officiously explained as I marched ahead, letting the group hold back to apply this sage wisdom to the raptor circling less than fifty feet over their heads.

And, do you know, it was several years before one of the members of that group brought to my attention that the alleged Red-tailed was in reality a perfectly identifiable Osprey.

Funny. I'd never really noticed that bright sunlight diffusing through an Osprey's tail has a reddish cast.

I'm not the only birder who makes errors, and some of the ones I've seen would be worthy of even my own worst efforts. I recall a nature center director who was adamant that the bird in the scope was a Great Egret right up until the point it lifted off the refuge's boundary sign, transforming itself into an adult Herring Gull.

I recall one of North America's best-known, and best-loved hawk watchers, who ushered me to a spotting scope set up on a "Peregrine" that was sitting on a distant tree line.

"An adult," he pointed out. "You can see the white breast moving."

It took a while for me to work through the inconsistencies. Like why the bird was perched so low. Like why the bird wasn't better defined. Like why the bird only moved when the wind was blowing. And it took me a little longer before I concluded that honesty was the best policy and pointed out that the adult Peregrine seemed to me to be sunlight shining through wind-whipped leaves.

All of these misidentifications were, of course, verifiably corrected. Some misidentifications aren't.

One of my all-time favorites involves a cluster-blunder committed by a host of pelagic birders. It was February and sixty degrees, and we were off the coast of New Hampshire.

I know this sounds impossible, but it's true.

Right off the bow, a bird was spotted that offered the eighty-odd trip members a better-than-average look at what I (and several friends) assessed to be a reasonably straightforward alcid species.

In something under thirty seconds, the bird was identified as a "Razorbill!" . . . "Murre" . . . "Dovkie!" . . . "Puffin." Bear in mind that only one of these identifications can be correct.

A runner sent down by the trip organizer advised that [the organizer] "will accept nothing less than puffin on that one."

"Oh boy, I got four Lifers out of that one," one trip-goer summarized. "Let's find some more."

Me? I thought it was a perfectly identifiable Dovkie myself. But then I'm not the world's best birder. And like I said, I've been wrong before.

Talkin' around a Sighting

[Scene: *A typical mudflat, at a typical coastal hotspot, with a typical assortment of gulls, terns, shorebirds, discarded tires, Styrofoam floats, and beer bottles. Poised behind spotting scopes are three typical birders who know each other but who arrived in separate cars.*]

Tim. Oh, my gosh.

Bill. What?

Tim. Oh, my GOSH!

Bill. WHAT?!

Tim. Are you looking at what I'm looking at?

Bill. [*Chuckling*] N-n-o. Obviously not.

Tim. That plover on the left. Second bird from the right-most dowitcher. Do you have it, Saul?

Saul. [*Pensive*] Yes. I've been studying it.

Bill. You mean the golden plover?

Tim. Yes . . . but look close. See the problem? It's not right.

Bill. What's not right?

Tim. Well . . . look at the flanks. They're all white except for some black.

Bill. It's August. The bird's molting.

TIM. Well . . . look at the stance. It's kind of erect but with a hunched quality, and the body is round but with a definite sense of squarishness about the head, middle, and tail . . . THERE. Did you see *that*?

BILL. See what? The bird scratching its neck? What of it?

TIM. Everything! American Golden-Plovers hardly ever drop their shoulders to scratch and never so much that it really looks like that's what they're doing. This bird clearly dropped its shoulder like a shopper laden with packages pushing their way through a revolving door. I've *never* seen an American Golden-Plover project a shopperesque GIZZ like that. Have you, Saul?

SAUL. [*Pensive*] Hmmm.

BILL. You're saying this is a Pacific Golden-Plover?

TIM. No . . . I think . . . I mean . . . well . . . I mean, I *think* that we should consider the possibility that this is something really, *really interesting*; something that is more in line with transoceanic vagrant than . . .

BILL. [*Breaking in*] ARE YOU SAYING THIS IS A EUROPEAN GOLDEN-PLOVER?

TIM. No, I'm saying that there's enough that's different about this bird that makes the possibility of European Golden-Plover worth considering and that we shouldn't rule anything out before we've studied the bird and considered all the things that don't seem right for American or Pacific Golden-Plover. That's what I'm saying.

BILL. [*Rolling his eyes, disgusted*] It looks about like every other molting golden plover I've ever seen. Saul, tell him. Do you see anything about this bird that makes you think it's anything but an American Golden-Plover in alternate plumage going into the first stages of molt?

SAUL. Well . . .

BILL. [*Not waiting for an answer*] There, you see. There is no accepted record for European Golden-Plover in the state, and only one record south of the Canadian Maritimes. So it can't be European Golden-Plover. That's impossible.

SAUL [*Continuing*] . . . What's interesting about this bird is the squarish shape of the head and smallish bill. The legs are stocky, the body thick, and the wing tips hardly extend much beyond the tail. Also, the white border separating the black underparts and the wings and the undertail coverts are lightly marked but not blotchy or broken, and the back pattern is finely flecked with gold, not coarsely patterned.

[*There is silence while the three birders study the bird and Bill and Tim consider Saul's analysis.*]

BILL. You know, it's funny, but I did notice that fine pattern on the back of this bird when I first set up but didn't say anything because the light was coming in from a funny angle. I even thought about the possibility of European Golden, but I've never seen one and didn't want to say anything until I could get some more on the bird, then it moved deeper into the flock.

TIM. Well, I think European Golden is a definite possibility here—but, you know, now that I've had time to study it, there are some things about the bird that are beginning to trouble me. See, American Golden Plover always remind me of Britney Spears leaning against the hood of 1964 Mustang convertible, eating Girl Scout cookies, while this bird is closer to Rosie O'Donnell sitting on a bench in a train station and eating gummy bears. You see what I mean?

BILL (*Looking away from his scope, studying Tim the way Adam might have regarded Eve after announcing that dessert would be apple turnovers*). What?

TIM. But what *really* bothers me about this bird is that speckling on the back. It's certainly not typical of American Golden-Plover—more like light leaking through a 16-oz. can of tomato puree that's been shot at close range with a full pattern of No. 9 shot than a seat cover that's been perforated over a half-hour period by a two-year-old wielding a model of a twin-engine P-38 fighter, which *is* classic for both American and Pacific Golden-Plover. But, see, the gold is duller! More like the crust from the end piece of a day-old Italian roll illuminated by the vanity light in a Dodge pickup than like a Rolex watch catching the last rays of sunlight through a window seat as your plane banks on its final approach to O'Hare in mid-December. You see what I mean, don't you, Saul?

SAUL. [*Pensive*] Hmmm.

BILL. Well, I'm going to start taking notes and doing a sketch. Are we all agreed that the bird has short legs and that the primaries don't project much beyond the tail?

TIM. Actually, I think the legs are more medium-length than short—more closely proportioned to the spare, sturdy, no-nonsense index finger of a ginsu chef or the middle finger of a New York cab driver than, say, the slim, dexterous pinky of a concert cellist or the elongated, double-jointed middle digit of an MG mechanic. You know, to be perfectly frank, the more I look at this bird, the more I am brought to think of an Idaho baked potato on stilts, which is exactly the impression I have of American Golden-Plover in juvenile plumage just after they arrived but before . . .

Hmmm.

Truth and Consequences

(At the Bird Lister's Ignominious Meeting)

The public address system screeched. Several folding chairs protested the weight of their human occupants and fell silent. The man at the podium adjusted the microphone and said:

"Ladies and Gentlemen and members of Bird Lister's Ignominious. My name is Neelie Gotumall and I'm a lister."

"Hi, Neelie," the crowd intoned.

"I see lots of old and new faces this evening. Before getting on to club business, I'm going to open up the mike. Anyone care to bare their souls in return for a little support?"

"How about you, sir?" he said, addressing a man in the first row—who stood, sighed, and mounted the podium. The face was a study in despondency.

"My name is Seymore Thanyou. And I'm a lister."

"Hi, Seymore," the crowd encouraged.

"I'm not out of control. At least I didn't think I was out of control. But last Saturday I missed my daughter's wedding because I went to chase the Spoon-billed Sandpiper. And it just about broke her heart. And it probably cost me my marriage. And I . . . I didn't even get th-the b-b-bird," he sputtered through a throat full of tears.

"Ohhhh," the crowd groaned.

"It's still showing," a club member promised. "Try again."

"Only fifty percent of marriages succeed these days," another member advised. "Promise you'll make the next one."

"Tell your wife you were trying to save money by seeing the bird here instead of flying all the way to Hong Kong. Tell her the savings would have underwritten the cost of the wedding."

The man nodded gratefully. "Thank you all so very much," he said. "That's great advice." He left the podium and a woman took his place.

"My name is Lotta Ticks," she said. "And I'm a lister."

"Hi, Lotta," the crowd chanted.

"I was all right as long as I stayed in North America," she said to the floor. But then I started World Listing and . . . well . . . pretty soon I was booking back-to-back tours to opposing ends of the planet and traveling to places even Rand McNally's never heard of."

"We're not rich," she continued. "I ran through all our savings," she said in a whisper. "I cashed in the IRAs. I've borrowed money from everyone who'd say yes, mortgaged the house, embezzled money from my parent's estate . . . "

"I'm in debt up to here," she said, looking at the crowd, pointing to the ceiling. I'm booked on a tour to Papua, New Guinea. I can't pay the balance. And there are still over thirty endemics I need there."

"Ohhhh," the crowd groaned.

"Just write a check," a member suggested. "You'll be on tour before it bounces. Worry about it later."

"For long-term financing, apply for a bunch of airline credit cards. Pay your debts off on one card, then shuffle the monthly balance between cards. You'll buy time and get lots of free air miles for trips."

"Wow," the woman said. "Those are great ideas. You people are terrific."

Another man took the podium. He was smiling.

"Hi. My name is Morris Better. And I'm a lister."

"Hi, Morris," they sang.

He continued strongly. "I'm not in financial straits and I'm not in social arrears but, I *do* have this problem and I want to set the record straight."

"See," he continued, "when the Whiskered Tern showed up, I went to the spot and the birds all flushed. I put my binoculars on the flocks but . . . well . . . I mean, I saw the flock. But I didn't actually see the bird."

His smile was the only one in a room that had grown ominously quiet.

"You counted it?" a voice wanted to know.

"Yes," the man said.

"On your Life List?" another club member demanded.

"Uh, yes. See, I've thought about this and I'm here to . . . "

"You counted that bird on your Life List," a female club member shouted, standing. "And at last year's Christmas Party you had the gall to tell me your Life List was one better than mine!"

"Yeah. I'm sorry. See, that's why I'm . . ."

"You bastard!" she screamed. "You lying, hypocritical, unprincipled bastard!"

Other people were on their feet, shouting now (and "bastard" was the kindest castigation being flung at the podium). The club moderator tried to restore order but failed. The man at the podium made a break for the rear entrance—but the idea was late in coming.

The police report in the local paper stated only that a club meeting at the local VFW hall had ended in a scuffle. One man was taken to the emergency room to remove the pages of bird names that had become affixed to his body with a hot, tarry substance. No charges had been filed and names were being withheld pending the results of an investigation.

The next club meeting would be one week hence, as scheduled.

Something Stringy about This

This essay is about "stringers."

> STRINGER, n. One whose bird sightings are stringy or suspect.

Every state has its stringers. They are celebrated for their audacity. They help define and sanctify the pure and honest birders...

"Oh, right, now [name deleted], *he's* a stringer (implication being you are not)."

. . . and help pass the time while everyone is waiting for the Little Stint to show up (and conversation relating to most birding tours taken and the newest thing in optics has dried up).

What makes a stringer? There are several key attributes.

First, while part of birding's social and information network, they always bird alone or in the company of someone who is less experienced.

Second, they habitually locate uncommon-to-rare birds (that nobody else seems able to find) with a frequency that humbles the efforts of other equally skilled birders and defies all odds.

Third, when you meet them in the field, they habitually tell you that you should have been there "five minutes ago" because they just had a [insert something improbable].

Fourth, their signature expression is: "It couldn't have been anything but" (translation: I got a glimpse of a bird but couldn't really tell what it was).

Fifth, when their names are mentioned to a group of birders, everyone rolls their eyes.

Sixth, they don't realize they are stringers.

But these are merely the attributes of a stringer. They say nothing about the roots of this malediction.

It would be easy to say that stringers are just birders who are liars and be done with it. For the most part, this isn't so. I believe that stringers really, truly believe that they saw what they say they saw. There are exceptions. I heard of one young birder whose sightings grew increasingly suspect. Confronted, he confessed to fabricating sightings because his father was opposed to his birding—until his son started getting his name in print in the birding journals. The kid figured that so long as he kept his name on the charts, his father would acquiesce to his hobby.

But *most* stringers believe that their sightings are legitimate. Stringers tend to be skilled and knowledgeable birders. They understand the cause-and-effect relationship between habitat and species, bird movement and temporal distribution.

They go to, say, a tidal wetlands in their Christmas Bird Count territory at dawn. They know that Black Rail breeds here, has even (on very rare occasions) been recorded in winter. They know that Black Rail would be a real coup at the roundup and that they should be attentive to . . .

ANDOHMYGOSH THAT WAS A SMALL BLACK RAIL THAT JUST RAN ACROSS THE CREEK. COULDN'T HAVE BEEN ANYTHING BUT. HOLLYCRAMOLY! JUST GOES TO SHOW YOU HOW IMPORTANT IT IS TO BE PREPARED.

So stringers are knowledgeable birders whose imagination gets the better of them, or individuals whose standards of acceptance are not as stringent as the norm? Both, in part. They are also birders who seek to anchor or elevate their standing among other birders through their sightings (otherwise, amassing stringy sightings would be as satisfying as cheating at solitaire).

So? So the reason there are stringers is that the birding community supports them. You heard me. We'd tip the authorities off to the identity of a mass murderer, we confront the neighbor whose dog pees on our begonias, but when your local stringer tells you he or she just had a Sooty Albatross off Long Island . . .

"Couldn't have been anything but!"

. . . we say: "Hmmmm."

Anybody who can turn a juvenile Northern Gannet into a Sooty Albatross can certainly mistake "Hmmmm," for affirmation.

That's right. We are (as they say in the substance-abuse environment) enablers. We are partners. We are those who hear the tree falling in the forest.

Stringers can't exist without us any more than birding could exist without a community of birders and a foundation of sightings that are fundamentally honest and accurate. We define them.

They help define us—and the line between stringers and non-stringers is probably not as sharp as most of us like to think or pretend. (By the way, the guy who tried to turn a Virginia Rail into a Black Rail under the catalytic influence of poor light and predisposition was me. Sometimes you forget how small and dark Virginias are).

So that makes me a stringer?

No, I don't think so. I mean, I believe that what I saw is what I said I saw. But then one of the attributes of a stringer is that they don't know they are stringers. And nobody in the birding community would tell me if I were.

Ridiculous. I'm *certain* I'm a careful, honest observer . . .

Couldn't be anything but.

Binocular Reality

I just opened today's mail—the bulk of which was third-class invitations targeting my concern for the environment. One told me that unless I acted now, the *blank-blank* was doomed. Another let me know that membership guaranteed me a spiffy day pack. A third was from a bank boasting that a portion of any transaction made with their Visa card would help birds.

Now, I'm not saying that many environmental organizations are not worthy of your support. Or that financial institutions don't want to save the planet. Or that I want to cut the U.S. Postal Service out of much-needed revenue. I'm just saying that if safeguarding the planet seems important, I've got another idea.

Give someone you know a pair of binoculars. Make the natural world intimate and make it real.

The problem is estrangement. We, as members of modern society, have become divorced from nature. We get up in the closeted confines of our homes, drive to work in climate-controlled vehicles, spend eight to ten hours cooped up in an artificial workplace, drive home, turn on the tube, and go to bed.

On weekends we cut the lawn (a habitat that is about as natural as a corn field) or go to the mall (whose common area is an artificial vestige of the natural habitat that used to be there).

No birds. No forests. No excitement. No intimacy. Nothing but insular routine.

Cut through the routine. Give someone the optical bridge that will link them to the natural world.

GIVE SOMEONE A PAIR OF . . .

Here's my theory. Here's why I think binoculars vault the barriers erected within the most suburban-deadened mind, opening a portal to the natural world. We (meaning everyone) start life as bundles of neural receptors linked to the outside world by sensory organs—ears, nose, skin, and, particularly, eyes. As we are lying there in the crib, the whole universe—sound, light, color, movement—is crashing in on our awareness. It's incredible. It's overwhelming. It's WOW!

To keep all this WOW from overloading the system, we sleep a lot—but between naps, we integrate the world into a cognitive framework, a sort of sensory blueprint to the universe. In time, everything falls into place: distance, morning light, the color red, wet diapers, Mom, the treachery of stairs, the sky, school buses, dentists, mortgages. It stops being overwhelming. In fact, it all becomes routine.

Then, one day (while you're cutting the grass) your neighbor hands you a pair of binoculars. You raise them to your eyes . . . and this magic instrument bores a hole right through your cognitive framework, blowing you right back to an infant brain stem.

WOW! You start panning around. Looking at things for the first time again. Rock . . . tree . . . toolshed. ("Huh," you think, "toolshed needs paint.") Then something catches your eye, something animate, something alive. You bring the binoculars to bear . . . and *gasp*.

It's so beautiful, you think. It's so alive. Look how it walks. Look how it stops and cocks its head. Look how it drives its yellow bill into the lawn and tugs and tugs and tugs at that pink, pink worm.

Why, you wonder, have you never noticed anything so wonderful before?

It's because you've never looked at an American Robin through binoculars before.

That's why.

WOW! And WOW is very alluring. WOW is very addictive. Once you get a taste of it, once is not enough. If binoculars give robins a cerebral punch, imagine what will happen to the optically opened mind when those binoculars fall upon a Blue Jay . . . a goldfinch . . . an iridescent starling . . .

A CARDINAL! Red and crested with black, black, beady eyes.

OH, WOW!!!

Once the birds of the backyard blow holes through your preconceptions, why, you have to start going afield—to parks and neighborhood woodlots, to sanctuaries and refuges, to Point Pelee, Ontario, and Ecuador, and to an intimacy with wetlands and rainforests and migrant traps—to see Green-winged Teal and Prothonotary Warblers and Resplendent Quetzals.

Incidentally, you can give people a bird feeder and give them a taste of WOW. But a bird feeder isn't going to get them a quetzal. It isn't going to save much more than the corner hedge.

Saving planets beats saving hedges. So buy them binoculars. Once people become intimate with nature, they become protective of it. If enough people become protective, environmentalists will constitute a majority.

When this happens the *blank-blank* won't be doomed. People will don backpacks and take to the woods (instead of the malls), using their bank cards to shop by mail, saving land that would otherwise be transformed into shopping centers.

WOW!

Circus genitalia

It was autumn. I was sitting atop the North Lookout of Pennsylvania's Hawk Mountain Sanctuary. Before me was the ridge top that serves as a pathway in the sky for migrating hawks. Around me, fellow hawk watchers. In front of me, two who were aspiring.

You could tell they were beginners because the optics they were using were of very poor quality. You could tell they were beginners because their field guide was utterly unsuited for identifying hawks in flight (so every passing Turkey Vulture was the catalyst for much page flipping and heated debate).

They might have been beginners, but like most of us who have been bitten by the hawk-watching bug, they were serious.

It was warm, the day's flight slow. Still, I was determined to find a hawk or two and, as often happens when determination goes head to head with low probability, determination wins out. I did find a bird. *W a a a a y* out there. Even with the advantage afforded by very fine optics (and very young eyes), it was only the suggestion of the shadow of a bird that materialized and dematerialized in the heat waves.

"I've got a bird," I announced. Off the slope of 'One.'" In front of me I could see the couple bring their shared pair of binoculars to bear. First one then the other tried, but neither could locate the bird. Frustrated, both of them stared back at me (wondering whether I wasn't perhaps just making it up).

I wasn't. There really was a bird out there and I was deeply engaged in meeting the next challenge. Pinning a name to it.

As the form drew closer, what had been the suggestion of a

bird became the suggestion of a hawk and then the suggestion of a certain kind of hawk. The wings were long, the V-shaped tilt to the wings real, not imagined, and despite the lack of wind, the bird's flight was unsteady, tippy, the mark of a light, buoyant bird of prey. Added to these clues was color. The hawk was pale, not dark, so *not* a Turkey Vulture.

"It's a 'Marsh Hawk,'" I asserted, sticking my neck out.

The couple in front of me redoubled their efforts, scanning frantically—but it was no use. Their optics and their inexperience were against them. This time, when they turned around, they glowered.

The bird left the ridge, starting off across the valley. Its course would not ferry it within half a mile of us. I held it in my glasses, held it because it was a hawk, a bird of prey, and nothing is more gratifying than pinning a name to a distant bird of prey. I believed this then. I believe it today. Everyone should be fortunate enough to have an obsession as obsessive as mine.

Midway across the valley, a vagrant gust of wind turned the bird on its side, exposing pure white underparts. Young harriers are cinnamon below; females tawny and brown. But the adult male, the beautiful and elusive "gray ghost," is white.

"It's an adult male!" I shouted. "Adult male!" The bird was, and remains, among my favorite birds.

At this the gentleman in front of me dropped his binoculars, threw up his hands, raised his eyes to heaven, and, leaning over, whispered to his wife: "I can't believe this son-of-a-bitch behind us. I can't even *find* this bird and he can see its *genitals*."

Fact: even with great binoculars, you can't see a migrating raptor's genitals.

Fact: if your objective is pinning a name to the bird, with good optics and a field guide geared up for the identification of distant hawks in flight, you don't have to see them.

Almost Ivory

One winter long ago I came as close as anyone will ever come again to finding an Ivory-billed Woodpecker in New Jersey. The expedition lasted several weeks, and I'll tell you plainly that the bird I sought was not an Ivory-billed—a bird whose last confirmed sighting in North America occurred in the 1950s. What I sought was Pileated Woodpecker, a smaller cousin, but one that shares much commonality with Ivory-billed, including this:

To that point in my life, I'd not seen *either* species. They lived as equals in my mind. This is how it is with birds that have thus far eluded you. Being a birder yourself, I'm sure you understand.

During my search I often found evidence of my prize. Oblong windows chiseled so deep in living trees that the trees glowed with back lit sunlight, wood chips the size of half dollars carpeting the snow.

Coming upon these chiseled portals, I would marvel at their size. Staring at the scattered shards, my heart would pound—with elation because I'd come so close, with despair because I'd come too late.

The despair was exaggerated of course. Insofar as finding Pileated Woodpeckers was concerned, I'd arrived at just the right time (in history). A century before, Pileated Woodpeckers were hardly less common than Ivory-billed Woodpeckers in my home state of New Jersey, their numbers since diminished, maybe extinguished, by near-total deforestation. In *Birds of New Jersey*, published in 1896, Pileated is unreferenced. In *Birds of the New York City Region*, published in 1923, the bird is "rumored" still to exist in the forested regions of extreme northwestern New Jersey.

But by the middle of this century, with forests rebounding, there were once again Pileated Woodpeckers in New Jersey's woodlands. All I had to do was find one.

I felt like Arthur Allen wading through the swamps of Louisiana's Singer Tract in search of North America's rarest woodpecker. I approached every turn in the trail with anticipation and, rounding it, looked forward to the next.

Until one day I heard a measured thump that had nothing to do with the sound of boots. I quickened my pace and the thumping got louder. I ran until the sound of the working bird and the thump of my heart were one.

Halfway up a hillside, a shower of wooden shards was falling onto the snow. Through raised binoculars I glimpsed the bird itself. Golden-eyed and red-crested, it peered at me from behind a massive trunk, then, spreading its great black-and-white wings, it flew. That was all the vision my weeks of effort had gained—but it was vision enough.

Later that night, after the journal entry was written, after the check mark was etched with a flourish next to the appropriate name, it occurred to me that I never really saw the bird's bill. Never saw it at all!

I know what logic and prudence dictate. The bird could not have been anything but a Pileated Woodpecker. On the other hand, to admit total certainty would be less than honest. I was not certain then; I am, these many years later, less confident now. With as much glee as honest regret, I am forced to admit that the bird's identity must always enjoy a measure of uncertainty. I will never honestly know whether that bird, so briefly seen, was the Pileated I anticipated or the Ivory-billed I did not.

As a birder, I'm sure you'll sympathize and understand.

Hearing

It took an Englishman to teach me to hear. His name was Jeff Delve. He had just flown in from England, then been whisked into a car and told that despite the late hour and his lack of sleep, he wasn't going to be ushered to a bed. He was, instead, going on the World Series of Birding, where he would be subjected to twenty-four hours of nonstop birding.

"OK," he said.

First light found us straddling an elevated railroad bed flanked by upland forest and overgrown fields, hardwood swamps and riparian meadows. As the day dawned, all the voices of the birds of a New Jersey spring rose to greet it, the voices whose joined elements are the sound of the Dawn Chorus.

"Song Sparrow," one of my teammates shouted.

"Begins with three identical notes," I counseled.

Jeff, his face the picture of concentration, nodded.

"Blue-winged Warbler!" another team mate exclaimed, " . . . and Golden-winged."

"Blue-winged. *Beee-buzzz,*" I coached. "Sounds like an asthmatic's inhaled and exhaled breath." Golden-winged. "Similar, but chokes on the buzz. *Bee-buzz, buzz, buzz.*"

Jeff nodded. "What is that background cacophony?" he wanted to know.

"Robins," I said.

The sounds came faster now. Snatches of song that surfaced in an audio-maelstrom.

"There. Towhee! Says his name."

A nod.

"Over there. Phoebe! Says his name."

A nod.

"In the back. Least Flycatcher! Dry, emphatic, *che-bek*! repeated over and over. Got it?"

A half nod. A nod given out of politeness. I realized that Jeff wasn't listening, wasn't sorting anymore. He was, instead, hearing. He was hearing it *all*.

We Americans take the sound of birds on a morning in spring for granted. But in many parts of the world, the voices in the Dawn Chorus are fewer, the performance not so grand. But even on this continent, the touring time for the Dawn Chorus is short. April, May, June (for the most part); March and July in some places. Then the tour ends. Nesting season over, birds rest their voices until next season.

There are cassettes and CDs and videos that help identify the voices in the chorus. If you love the songs of birds, you'll love them more when you recognize the voices of individual singers. But if all you want to do is hear, as my friend Jeff was hearing, then stop listening and start experiencing. Get up. Go out. Hear it.

Jeff's face was no longer contorted by concentration. It was serene and it glowed—maybe from the color rising in the sky, maybe from some light within. And if souls are tuning forks that vibrate in concert with great natural forces, his was in tune, harmonized with the sound of his first Dawn Chorus.

New Eyes

It might have been fortune. It might have been a snatch of color, leaking through the leaves, tugging at the corner of my eye.

But now, with time to reflect, I think it was some sixth sense that turned my head toward the island of trees. And stripped away the shadows. And brought my eyes to bear on the ocher-colored face framing eyes that glowed with sleepy malice. The eyes of a Great-horned Owl.

It was a shock, I don't mind saying. Seeing the jug-sized bird a scant thirty feet away. Eye level! Unstirring. Cloaked within the latticework of branches that served as its roost.

I could not believe my fortune. All my life I've stalked Great-horned Owls, hoping for a look that satisfies, and been treated to nothing but retreating forms and empty air. Every time I close on some tattletale band of crows, every time I stalk some pine grove where pellets abound, the birds retreat.

Great-horned Owls are shy, the books all said. They're "witchy," says my coworker (and coauthor of *How to Spot An Owl*) Pat Sutton.

But now I had one. Dead to rights. Trapped on an island of trees, surrounded by open marsh. A Great-horned Owl. Trapped for my viewing pleasure.

Smugly I stared into the eyes, dominating the owl with a victorious smile. But the owl didn't flinch, didn't acknowledge my mastery of the situation at all. In fact, the bird just stared back, his eyes locked with mine; not at all what I expected.

Maybe the bird was sick, my mind offered as a possibility.

Maybe it was injured (*must* be injured to behave so oddly), or perhaps it was starving.

But the bird didn't look sick, or injured, or famished. In fact, it looked as if looking at me was precisely what it wanted to do. Which was odd, even disquieting, in a creature so shy, unless . . .

Unless, my imagination proposed, Great-horned Owls weren't really shy at all. What if it was just a game that the birds had played with would-be observers. Hide and seek; fly when stalked.

What if owls, when undetected, stood their ground. Savoring each and every oblivious human passage.

Sizing us up!

I might have passed hundreds, even thousands, of Great-horned Owls in my life. Had my privacy stripped away as easily as the devil harvests souls. Been coolly appraised by eyes that pin their gaze upon other warm-blooded creatures just before pinning them to the snow.

A silent glide. A sudden impact. Nothing between my being alive and my being prey except my superior size.

But trapped in the scrutiny of the bird, I didn't feel very superior. I began to consider how many rabbits must have seen what I was seeing now, knowing it was the last thing they would ever see. I found myself trying to recall the upper size limit of Great-horned Owl prey, found myself wondering why this owl had decided to break the rules and let me see him, and did this mean that he was the sort of owl who played fast and loose with all the rules of engagement?

And what were those rules? What was requisite behavior for an owl that lets itself be seen? Did this mean . . . ? Was I then . . . ?

I found myself deciding, suddenly, to walk on. Busy schedule, you know. Deadlines to meet. Dinner to make.

I found, as I rounded the corner, that my heart was racing at a rabbit's pace and that hairs on the back of my neck twitched.

I looked at the woodlands flanking the road. Looking with new eyes. Looking for hidden eyes. Realizing suddenly what every successful rabbit knows at the core of his being: woodlands are never as empty as they seem.

Intimate

The perch that was empty became full—full of beak, full of breast, full of beady, black eye. The intimacy was so intimate I could see my reflection in the bird's eye.

In real, unaided life, a human-to-bird encounter this close would have been impossible. Birds, after all, have wings. Cross the invisible line that defines their flush distance and they leave.

But with a spotting scope, all the rules governing birds and intimacy are broken. At 60x power, at a distance of twenty feet, my functional proximity was a heart-stopping *four inches*, was microscopic!

"Wow," I breathed, silently and without reason. After all, there was plate glass and a comfortable distance between me and the bird. As far as the bird was concerned, I was playing by the rules. Calm, unperturbed, the bird performed as though I wasn't even there.

Spotting scopes are not the primary tool of birding—that title goes to the binocular. And spotting scopes have, traditionally, been instruments for serious birders—high-magnification tools that permit users to identify birds at extreme distances or discern minute details that separate look-alike species.

Until recently, most spotting-scope manufactures didn't give much thought to the close-focus capability of their instruments. Twenty-five, thirty, even forty feet was considered good enough.

Ah, but then birders began being seduced by intimacy. If close looks were good, closer was better, and in-your-face was best of all. Slowly, manufacturers came to understand that birds that beg to be studied are not necessarily time zones away. Sometimes they may be compellingly close. Seductively close.

With a scope that focuses down to fifteen feet or less, they fill mind and soul.

Wow.

Captivated, I watched as the bird dipped his bill into the pile of seed, extracting a smooth, black cylinder. Fascinated, I noted how he massaged the seed from the shell, inhaled my offering, thanked me with the gift of his presence.

Each and every feather seemed drenched in wine. Sunlight played off the ivory-colored bill and skipped across the night-black surface of his eye. I could see every move, every feature, every living, breathing nuance of the bird that had come to my offering of seed.

"House Finches are awesome," I thought. "If a male cardinal shows up, I'll have to look away or go blind."

Birding Products for the Twenty-first Century

I don't know whether you've noticed, but it seems like every hobby (except birding) boasts a cornucopia of products designed to meet every real and presumed avocational need. Go to any garden, boat, or hunting and fishing show, and you'll find an array of stuff enthusiasts can't live without that mantles entire city blocks.

Maybe birding hasn't been around long enough for entrepreneurs to sniff out the market. Maybe those people who have raised the cost of catching a largemouth bass to $190 per inch feel that birders don't want or need anything but binoculars and a field guide.

But maybe product analysts just lack insight. So here, for the benefit of investors, venture capitalists, and (ultimately) those of us who will buy all of these toys, are my ideas for products that birders cannot live without. Products like a corrective lens that fixes the blurring you get every time you look at a bird through a car windshield. Just slip the frame over the objective lenses of your binoculars (or in the contact lens version, over the ocular lenses) and . . .

THE *BLUR* IS *GONE*!

Because windshield curvature varies among automobile makes and models, it stands to reason that lenses will require a prescription fitting. This is good because when you find yourself in a situation in which you need to fall back on the classic excuse that you didn't get a "good enough look" at the bird because you were "looking through the windshield," you can instead say that you need to get your prescription changed.

Speaking of binoculars, one option I know that every birder will want is a "temporal adjustment knot"—a fixture that will let you set the image back to that moment when the branch (which is still vibrating) held the bird that, according to smug witnesses, "just flew."

Or how about a filter that will automatically block out Herring Gulls at Niagra Gorge, Snow (but not Ross's) Geese at Bombay Hook, or Yellow-rumped Warblers at Cape May?

How about a binocular barrel with a hinge—so that aging birders can look up without craning their necks skyward? I'm talking about a product that could wipe out warbler neck in our lifetime.

Something that frustrates me is the frequency with which field guides need replacing. Every time the checklist committee of the American Ornithologists' Union adds a hyphen to a bird's name, my field guide becomes dated. So, why not market a "field guide conversion kit"—an adhesive-backed envelope filled with an assortment of hyphens and upper- and lowercase letters that can be affixed to the inside cover of a field guide?

Then, if Eyebrowed Thrush is ever changed back to Eye-browed Thrush, I can just reach into the envelope, extract a hyphen, and insert it in the proper place (instead of buying a new book). Or, if Common Black-Hawk ever reverts to Common Black Hawk, I can remove the hyphen and store it in the envelope.

Certainly every birder will want the walk-along tripod—a product that uses the latest in robotic technology to keep up with you (instead of having to be carried around like a cranky two-year-old). Deluxe models could be programmed to meet you at the mudflat.

The Big Day is, of course, fertile ground for product development. It is here, at birding's fringe, that human limits cry out for the sort of technological leverage that will shave time (and save vehicles).

To this end, I offer two products that will revolutionize the Big Day. First, a self-leveling dashboard that will keep coffee levels stable during hard cornering, making it finally possible for Big Day birders to ingest more coffee than they wear.

Of course, drinking all this coffee will present another problem. It will mean that Big Day birders will have to stop more frequently to divest themselves of processed coffee—a time-consuming and counterproductive business.

Which is why some surgical-instrument concern should hasten development of the Big Day Birding Catheter—a simple, sanitized tube that will tap kidneys that are working as hard as you are. Custom-fitted to run the length of the user's leg, the tubes will have a lever-controlled nozzle that may be switched to the open position when team members leave the vehicle, or, between stops, hooked up to a main line running through the car, allowing members to passively relieve themselves of processed coffee between sites.

Deluxe models might come with their own IV coffee drips—with lines color-coded for obvious reasons. Prescription required. Read instructions before use. FDA approval pending—and not at all certain.

Peenter Pan

You'll have to bear with me for this one, have faith that there is reason (if not rhyme) and that a twentieth-century poet, a goat-footed god, keyboard wizard Keith Emerson, and *Philohela minor* (the American Woodcock) really do have something in common.

Even if this juxtaposition lives only in a writer's mind.

You are familiar with American Woodcock, of course. The long-billed, bulging-eyed upland shorebird that resembles a meat loaf on a stick? It is shy and retiring. A wallflower in shorebird's clothing. But when the spark of spring strikes that lightning-rod bill, the birds go ballistic.

Lifting off from weedy, wood-fringed launch sites, climbing like a string-cut kite, the birds go aloft. As they ascend, they twitter like gym-rimming preteens at the St. Valentine's Day dance and spiral like a spring-maddened Pan.

That's Pan, mythological Greek god of woods and fields. Goat-footed pan whom e. (for Edward) e. (for Estlin) cummings once wrote into a poem that embodies the reckless, feckless, heart-skipping, foot-skipping, "puddle-wonderful, mudluscious" essence of . . .

"in Just—

spring"

God of woods and fields. Shorebird of fields and wooded edge. Get it? Do you grant that we have a match? Now factor in the cummings-coined term "mudluscious." A term *any* woodcock can relate to. Even the name *Philohela* means (in Greek, of course) "bog lover."

So now you understand about the poet and Pan. But what you may not know is that Pan had pipes. As he danced through spring-saturated fields, he played, and while the tune has been lost to antiquity, I imagine that it must have recalled the song of the American Woodcock.

No, not the twittering part. Twittering is the recourse of those too timid to dance. I'm talking about the full-blown love song of the American Woodcock, emitted when the birds reach the hormonally fueled peak of their climb then surrender to love and gravity.

The vocalizations turn giddy, mad! The song sounds like water dripping in a dream, communication satellites speaking in tongues, Pan's lips moving over his pipes in random fashion.

It sounds one heck of a lot like the tail end of a cut off an old E.L.&P. (that's E. for Emerson, L. for Lake, P. for Palmer, you pre-sixties/seventies or post-nineties readers) album. Group keyboardist Keith Emerson just let the Moog synthesizer have its head. The machine and the song spiral in a descending flood of electronic notes.

First time I ever heard a courting woodcock, it recalled that old E.L.&P cut.

So now you know how it is that the dance of the American Woodcock conjures the joined elements of poets, musicians, and gods in my mind. If this sounds too crazy for words, just remember that the woodcock's song is a melody (there are no words) and that getting crazy is precisely what spring is all about.

Now stop your twittering. Get up and dance.

The Trust of Jay

You could tell it was a Blue Jay of course. Despite the snow, despite the evening light that turned blue to slate, the silhouette was unmistakable. The hallmark crest was peaked, erect. The tail nicely rounded. And the bird's eyes? They were jet, dark as the winter night closing over the world. From a distance of fifteen feet they peered into mine.

I was coming home after an evening walk—looking forward to hot cocoa and a fire-warmed room. The Blue Jay had flown in and taken perch on the drooping branches of a pin oak. Both of us froze.

I'm not used to intimacy with birds. Insight, yes. Understanding, yes. Intimacy, no. For forty-three years, I've watched birds, studied them, enjoyed them—but the times during which they have opened their lives to me are few.

And to be perfectly honest, I wasn't on completely friendly terms with Blue Jays. Their habit of nest robbing disturbed me. Their brassy voices and raucous behavior were, at times, disenchanting. Their penchant for dominating the feeder and hogging the sunflower seed not endearing.

How many times had I seen them swoop down on my feeding tray, scattering smaller birds in their wake? They'd hop to the center of the tray like they owned it, and bolt down the choicest seed while other hungry minions waited their turn.

But I had to admit, this Blue Jay had me fascinated. What was it doing on this winter eve, while the snow fell and the world turned to shadow? What made him stand so long, so balefully long, like a truant caught in the act? Like a thief caught in the night watchman's beam? I wanted to know. I demanded an accounting.

Then, shyly, more like a newlywed taking to its bed than a brigand bound for booty, the bird half hopped, half flew into a closeting cluster of leaves and disappeared. Despite my presence, despite the risk, despite my ill-formed ill regard, the bird had gone to roost.

I stood for a minute or two, humbled by the trust the bird had shown. Then, with the snow turning my shoulders white, I continued home. Later, with my feet stretched in front of the fire and a cup of cocoa in my hands, I thought of the bird who had trusted me with his gravest secret, the secret of his sanctuary. More than by the cocoa, more than by the fire, I was warmed by this trust.

Ghost Writing

The book displayed on CMBO's bookstore counter was new (meaning it hadn't been there before). I grabbed a copy as I passed because a center director should keep abreast of things that happen in his nature center.

Maybe it was the early hour. Maybe it was because the room was pre-sunrise dark. For whatever reason, it was several steps before the title registered and before the realization hit home. The impact brought my feet to a stop and a smile to my face.

Wild America. The epic birding journey of Roger Peterson and James Fisher across North America, the *Moby Dick* of birding had finally been reprinted. Now birders wouldn't have to root around in musty used-book stores trying to locate a not-too-thumbed copy.

If you are not familiar with the book, you should be. It is the embodiment of birding, the adventure all birders emulate in their hearts and in their dreams. Some, like Kenn Kaufman (*Kingbird Highway*) and wife Linda and I (*The Feather Quest*), are lucky enough to have lived the dream through journeys of our own.

But my surprise and my pleasure were not founded on or limited to the book and its title—not strictly. Death has come between Roger Tory Peterson and his prolific writings. His words, freshly etched in the pages of newly titled books and articles in sundry periodicals, were the primary link between the patriarch of birding and his many students. On July 28, 1996, the link was broken . . . or so, until this moment, I had assumed.

But as the book in my hand proved, Roger was too great a figure to be stopped by something as trifling as mortality. His writing vaulted the void.

Ghost writing.

With this thought in mind, I strode over to the bookstore racks, looking for more evidence of immortality. Yes, there were the field guides—*Eastern Birds, Western Birds, Wildflowers* . . . There too were all the books bearing the proud boast FOREWORD BY ROGER TORY PETERSON. *The Complete Birder* . . . *The Birds of Massachusetts* . . .

Hawks in Flight!

At one time, a foreword by Peterson was near-mandatory. Any book that was tacit to birds or birding seemed diminished without his legitimizing touch. And Roger took pains to honor those many requests from hopeful authors, the ones seeking the sanctifying touch conferred by his writing a foreword.

He was birding's tribal chief. He felt honor-bound and duty-bound to write forewords when asked. I know this to be true. He told me so.

The man is gone. The words remain. And isn't that odd. Because if you look at words one way, as lines on paper, they seem so frail. But so long as there are printers who print and readers who read, those words and those lines will keep the door wedged open between this world and the next.

And who knows? Who is to say that the door doesn't open both ways? There are those who say it does.

If words ring true. If they engender in readers an echo. Who is to say where an echo may travel? Or how far? And whose celebrated ears may receive it?

Golden Wings

Suddenly . . . he wasn't there.

I mean HE was there. More there, more real, than he had ever been.

In life.

He just wasn't *there.*

On the bed. Where he lay. As if asleep. One unruly frock of hair draped across his forehead. Wife Ginny not far away, making sure everything was just so.

For a moment, he recalled the flicker he'd found as a youth on Old Swede Hill. A bird he thought dead that burst to life at the touch of a finger. He wished very much that he could feel that touch now—but it was not to be.

Roger Tory Peterson was dead.

"Good-bye, Ginny," he voiced across a widening gulf and a wall of light that was falling between them. "It's been wonderful."

And . . .

"It might be a good idea to cancel my appointments for tomorrow, don't you think?"

"And could you contact Houghton Mifflin and tell them to make sure someone watches the color quality when they go to press on the fifth edition?"

"And I think I saw a Pipevine Swallowtail in the butterfly garden, yesterday. You'll want to watch for it."

And there were many other worldly matters he wanted to discuss—both great and small—but the distance had grown too great now. All the bonds that bound the greatest teacher-naturalist the world has ever known to the world he had known were breaking.

There was only one strand left. One woven of love—for all that he in his eighty-seven years had loved. Along this strand, there was only time enough to say "good-bye."

And then someone said, "Hello."

"Hello," Roger replied, turning to find an earnest-looking angel heading his way. His robe was long, loose-fitting, and white. Wings, extended, tapered. Crown, golden; halo, full. Smile . . .

Be-a-tific.

In his hand was a scroll. On his shoulder a button that read: "Hi, my name is Bob. Ask me about Eternity."

"Dr. Peterson," the angel said. "Welcome to heaven. I've been assigned to you for today."

"I'm very pleased to meet you," said Roger, who had (like most of us) never seen an angel before.

"You know," Roger mused. "I've often observed that the only creatures with feathered wings are angels and birds. Is that true?"

"Quite true," the angel replied.

"Would you mind if I studied them?" Roger asked. "Ever since the time I reached out to touch a flicker that I thought was dead and it burst into life I've been fascinated by creatures that fly."

"Study them as long as you like," the angel invited.

"Beautiful," said Roger. "Do they work? I mean can you fly . . . or are they just for decoration?"

"Of course they work," said the angel. "Be hard to get around up here without them. In fact, these are special issue. Low camber, high aspect ratio.

"I'm usually assigned to Heralds. But I'm cross-training down here in Triage. Personnel said it would be a smart career move."

"You're a young angel, then?" Roger asked.

"Uh-huh. Here. Look at my feather edges. Pretty fresh plumage, wouldn't you say?"

"Yes," Roger noted. "Hardly any wear at all. And the edges of the coverts are pale. Is that characteristic of young angels?"

"Classic," said the angel. "Archangels have uniform coverts and shorter primaries. The plumage is whiter, too."

"This is fascinating," said Roger. "Are there any other color morphs? A dark morph, perhaps?"

A sudden cloud eclipsed the sun and there was a rumble of thunder.

"We don't discuss that up here," the angel replied.

"Oh," Roger said, retreating. Looking for some way to change the subject. Seeing the scroll in the angel's hand.

"Is that a summary of my life?"

"Yes, it is," the angel chimed.

"All of it? Roger asked. "Even the time I . . . "

"Everything. From the time you arrived late for Sunday Service at Jamestown's Holy Trinity Church (with muddy shoes and rumpled clothes, and the excuse that the birds were singing so beautifully) to the ice cream cone you sneaked during the World Series of Birding when Ginny wasn't there to stop you."

"I see," said Roger, trying to look more contrite than he felt. "But . . . in the balance, I've led a good life?"

"Exemplary," said the spirit. 'Angels High' as we say up here."

"Then, I've made it!" Roger exclaimed. "I'm in heaven."

At this point the angel's smile, which had been beatific, became strangely frozen. "Yes and no," he replied.

"What does that mean?" Roger demanded. "I thought that if you led a good life, you went to heaven."

"You do; you do," the angel soothed. "It's just that, well, I'm embarrassed to say that we're facing something of a demographic challenge at the moment."

"A challenge?" Roger challenged.

"To be frank, there's a housing shortage. You see, when the folks in long-range planning were making their growth estimates, there were a few miscalculations.

"First they overestimated the population-dampening effect of the bubonic plague. Then some genius projected that the Shaker religion was going to become a global fad. To top things off, during the potato famine three times as many lusty young Irish lads emigrated abroad as became priests. (A clerk inverted the fraction. Our population projections were based on a *celibacy* factor of 3:1).

"And while television *has* turned birth rates around, it's a classic example of too little, too late.

"The problem is temporary," the angel promised. "But until we can catch up with demand, we're returning all new arrivals back to earth."

"I guess that's all right," said Roger. "In fact, it's probably just as well. You know, I've not finished the fifth edition of my guide yet. And I've wanted for the longest time to try my hand at painting again and . . . "

Roger stopped when he saw the pained expression on the angel's face.

"Is something wrong?"

"Yes," the angel replied. "I forgot to mention that you can't go back as yourself. You can imagine the confusion it would cause. I'm here to help you find a temporary life until you're recalled.

"I'm *sure* we can find something that will please you, Dr. Peterson." And before Roger could reply, the angel whipped out another scroll and started running through the entries.

"Ah, here's something. A job at the Union Furniture Factory in Jamestown, New York. They need an artist to paint Chinese decorations on lacquered furniture."

"I don't think so," Roger said. "In fact, if I'm not mistaken, that's the job I left in 1925 to attend the Art Student League of New York. Haven't they filled it yet?"

"I guess not," the angel concluded. "Sure you're not interested?"

"Very sure," said Roger. "What else do you have?"

"Well, *here's* an opening at Houghton Mifflin. They're looking for an editor for a field guide series. The job's just been posted."

"That's the job I just left," said Roger.

"Oh," said the angel, "right. Well, how about . . . "

"Isn't there any listing for a bird artist or bird conservationist or birding spokesperson or something?"

"No, nothing under those titles . . . "

"Well, what *do* you *do* with people that you can't fit to a job?"

"We send them all back as attorneys," the angel replied.

"Oh," said Roger. "That explains a lot."

"I guess it does," the angel agreed.

"Why attorneys?" Roger wanted to know.

"It's a respectable profession, sort of in league with right vs. wrong, good vs. evil (themes that play real well up here)."

"I see," said Roger. "Well, I don't think I would make a very good attorney. Isn't there some alternative, a waiting list . . . or an appeals process?"

The angel was silent for a moment. And if Roger was more attentive, the silence would have been cause for disquiet. When the angel spoke, he whispered; but in the eternal silence of that world, his words came across as loud judgment.

"There is an appeals process," the angel spoke, as if quoting scripture.

"For those whose lives have moved humanity closer to the ideals of heaven,

"For those to whom respect is due by both heaven and earth.

"If you choose, your case can be reviewed by a panel of peers. Pass muster in *their* eyes and you'll gain heaven. Fail, and you'll be returned to earth to a life that inversely reflects the greatest triumph of your last.

"A full life, mind you! No early reprieve. And all the merit of the life you've just led is forfeited."

"Can you give me an example?" Roger asked.

"Richard Nixon," the angel offered.

"Yes?"

"Was reincarnated as a young law clerk in the office of Kenneth Starr."

"That doesn't sound so bad," said Roger.

"He was returned to life with a compulsive desire to see a Prothonotary Warbler."

"So?"

"Mr. Nixon's eyes are so packed with receptor cells for the color red, he can't perceive yellow."

"That's very sad," said Roger. And for a moment he thought maybe he'd just take that chair-painting job in Jamestown, New York. Then, perhaps because he was thinking about home, he recalled again the first time he went birding, up Old Swede Hill. And the flicker he came upon at the base of a tree that sprang to life at the touch of his finger, spreading wings that looked like they were forged of sunlight.

It was this contrast, between the bird that seemed dead and the one that sprang to life, that captured his eleven-year-old imagination. And spurred his life of accomplishment. And, not surprisingly, guided his decision now.

"I'll take my chances with the panel," Roger asserted. "I've tried to live a good life. I think I've made a difference. I can't imagine a panel denying me heaven because I wore muddy shoes to church or cheated on my diet. I think I've earned my wings.

"I do get wings, don't I?"

"You do get wings," the angel assured.

"As good as yours?"

"As good as the life you led," the angel promised. "Come with me."

They walked across a landscape that was as perfect as Eden was not. They may have walked a short time, or it may have been a long time (because there is no time in heaven). They came to a stop in what seemed to be a room.

In front of Roger was a bench and three opaque figures. Around him were shapes that walked the edge of recollection—people Roger felt certain he knew.

"Is it always so misty up here?" Roger asked.

"Shhh," the spirit cautioned.

"Dr. Peterson?" a voice intoned. A gentle voice that spoke English with a German accent.

"That's Albert Einstein," Roger gasped as the mist cleared, disclosing the tousled form of the century's greatest physicist. He was wearing a baggy, argyle robe with a hole in the sleeve and a soup stain down the front. He was regarding Roger with solemn eyes.

"Roger *Tory* Peterson," another voice echoed. A precise voice, spoken with command.

"That's General Douglas MacArthur," Roger whispered as the clearing mist revealed the chiseled form of the army officer who had served his country in three twentieth-century wars. He was dressed in a khaki robe with creases so sharp they cut the light of heaven. On his collar he bore the shadowy impressions of five stars.

"I thought you said I was to present myself to a panel of *peers*?" Roger demanded of his angel. "These are two of the greatest men in history."

The angel shrugged. "They are peers. Men of your century. Men of achievement. Men whose lives are a measure for the rest. You've already passed muster with heaven, Dr. Peterson. But you went for early admission and, now, you must make the grade with them. I never said it was going to be easy."

"Is this fellow really a bird watcher?" a third voice wanted to know. A British voice. The mist cleared to reveal a thin, intense man of forty or so, wearing a turtlenecked robe and a dark beret. He was smoking a cigarette and peering at Roger through wire-rimmed glasses.

"John Lennon," the angel whispered, anticipating Roger's question. "The Beatle, John Lennon. They like to have someone from the arts on these panels, and Aaron Copeland couldn't make it."

"I see," said Roger. "Well, I like the British—in fact, I once traveled with James Fisher, a British colleague, across North America. We wrote a book called *Wild America*. But I'm not a big fan of rock music."

"I wouldn't proclaim that loudly right now," the angel counseled.

"No, of course," Roger agreed, smiling up at half of heaven's claim to the Fab Four. "They allow smoking up here?"

"It's heaven," the angel said. "You can do anything you want. Besides, you can't die. But perhaps you should answer Mr. Lennon's question."

"YES, yes," said Roger. "I watch birds and many other things, too."

"I wrote a song about a bird once," said John Lennon. "Blackbird singing in the dead of night?"

"I don't believe I've heard it," Roger replied.

"Take these broken wings and learn to fly . . ." Lennon coaxed.

"I'm afraid not," Roger replied.

"All your life. You were only waiting for this moment to arrive?" John Lennon continued, and concluded, "Pretty poignant, wouldn't you say, Mr. Birdman?"

"Yes," said Roger, "assuming of course, you are referring to the European Blackbird, which is really a thrush, and not one of the New World blackbirds which are icterids and do not commonly sing at night."

The ex-Beatle took a drag of his cigarette and blew a smoke ring. "I guess you're a birder all right," he said.

"Dr. Peterson." It was the voice of Albert Einstein.

"Ve can have der discussion about birds another time, maybe, but now it is important for us to look at your life und see if vether you are qualified for early admission. First ve vill examine your achievements; den ve vill see vether maybe zere is somezing in your life that is not kosher. If you agree, say 'yah'."

"Yah," Roger agreed. "I mean yes."

"Gut," said the physicist. "I see zat you have tventy-zree academic degrees! Dat is a very impressive number. At vat universities did you teach?"

"I didn't teach at any universities," Roger admitted. "However, I was a counselor at Camp Chiwonki in Maine and later taught at the Rivers School outside of Boston. That's where I worked on my *Field Guide to the Birds*—it revolutionized the way people identify birds. My degrees are all honorary."

"I see," observed the physicist who revolutionized the way humanity looks at the universe. "Your degrees are honorary."

General MacArthur spoke next.

"Mr. Peterson, you were evidently of military age during the Second World War. I assume you served your country?"

"I did," Roger asserted.

"In which theater?" asked the man who commanded Allied operations in the Pacific.

"In both," said Roger. "By proxy." I was in the Army Corps of Engineers, stationed outside Washington. I developed a guide to enemy airplanes based upon my field guide to the birds."

"So you did not see action?" demanded the general.

"No," said Roger.

"But you held an officer's rank?"

"No. I was a private, sir."

"No more questions, Private Peterson," said five-star General Douglas MacArthur.

Now it was John Lennon's turn.

"Mr. Birdman. Did you ever make the cover of *Rolling Stone*?"

"Of what?" asked Roger.

"*Rolling Stone*," Lennon repeated.

"*Magazine*," the angel whispered.

"I don't recall," said Roger. "I've been interviewed by lots of writers for lots of publications, but I don't specifically recall that one."

"I see," John Lennon confided to the tip of his cigarette. "Don't recall ever being on the cover of *Rolling Stone*."

There was a short pause while the trio regarded their notes—time enough for Roger to lean over to the angel and ask, "How do you think it's going?"

"Shhh," the angel cautioned.

"Dr. Peterson," said Albert Einstein. "Is it fair to say that you regard your field guide der principle achievement of your life?"

"I do."

"Und in the first edition, you say zat zee idea vas from another book by Ernest Thompson Seaton—*Two Little Savages*, yah?"

"That's right."

"But in zee fourth edition, zere is no mention of zis. Vy is zis, and why, maybe, should I not sink zat it is because you sought not to give credit?"

This took Roger aback. "I have never tried to hide the fact that Seaton's display of ducks at a distance was the model I applied to all species. I've said this repeatedly. If it's not mentioned in the fourth edition, well, I guess after forty-five years I assumed everybody knew the story."

"I am sure it is as you say, Dr. Peterson, but to my old academic eyes, it is very curious. I must ask because *arrogance* is not a quality favored in heaven. Here even angels get der boot for it."

Roger tried to respond, but Douglas MacArthur cut him off.

"Private Peterson, I note that you've published four editions of this book and are working on another. Once, when asked why, you said, 'because it hasn't been done well enough, yet.' Private Peterson, are you perhaps succumbing to the sin of *pride*?"

Again, Roger was taken aback. "I'm more a perfectionist than I am prideful, General. I've always tried to use my talents to the best of my ability. In this I certainly take pride, but with my work I'm more apt to be critical."

"So you say," the general intoned, "but it has been my experience that prideful men sometimes put themselves above the will of heaven, the chain of command. You should know that it is *humility*, not *pride*, that wins points in heaven."

Now it was John Lennon's turn.

"Mr. Birdman, I see that you are an admirer of Canadian artist Robert Bateman's work. In fact, you once said that if you could paint like anyone else it would be like Robert Bateman. Could it be, Mr. Peterson, that you *envy* Robert Bateman?"

"NO!" said Roger. "Admire, yes. Envy, no. I appreciate his skill and like his style but wouldn't trade it for my own. I've had my own lifetime of achievements and enjoyed a measure of earned praise. I don't covet anyone else's achievements and I certainly don't want to be anyone but myself," he asserted—falling right into the trap.

"That sounds a lot like *pride* to me," said Douglas MacArthur.

"*Arrogance*, even," said Albert Einstein.

"I've heard enough," said John Lennon.

"Yah, it is time to vote," said Einstein.

"I don't think you'd have made a very good lawyer, Private Peterson," said Douglas MacArthur.

Roger sat as if stunned—which is not far from true. After all, it's not every day you die, have heaven denied, and have three of the most famous personalities of your century accuse you of arrogance, pride, and envy.

It was almost enough to instill *doubt*.

"You still have the option of taking the deferred entry plan," the angel whispered in his ear. "Just say that you've reconsidered. Nobody will think less of you. It won't even appear on your record. Trust me on this."

And Roger was tempted. It didn't seem right, and it didn't seem fair, but it sure seemed like the appeal was a failure . . . and it wasn't like he hadn't enjoyed painting furniture.

He stood to speak. He started to speak. He was about to take the angel's advice. And then his sense of rightness got in the way.

He decided to give the panel a piece of his mind! (and let the devil take the hind end!) when a voice he had not heard in over seventy-five years commanded:

"Roger, sit down."

A figure emerged from the mist and approached the trio on the bench. She was slight and freckled and had reddish hair. She stood as rigid as a yardstick and walked as straight as a ruled chalk line.

"Who is that?" the angel asked.

"That is . . ." said Roger.

"YOU ARE?" demanded Douglas MacArthur.

"I *am*," replied the figure, "Blanche Hornbeck, Roger's seventh-grade teacher. It was in *my* junior Audubon Club that Roger got his interest in birds. Didn't you, Roger?"

"Madam," admonished Douglas MacArthur, "this is highly irregular. This is not a trial. There is no call for witnesses. We are here only to decide whether this man has standing . . ."

"Exactly," said Miss Hornbeck. "It is a question of standing. And I suggest the three of you stand down and start listening because I see more projection than honest appraisal here."

"Madam," asserted the general, "I am not in the habit of taking orders."

"That's right, General," she said. "In fact, if memory and history serve, you disobeyed a direct order given to you by the President of the United States. An act of *pride* that may not have denied you heaven, but it sure cost you command of troops in Korea, didn't it?"

"Roger never lost a command. Did you, Roger?"

"No, Miss Hornbeck," Roger chanted.

"As for arrogance, Dr. Einstein, didn't you once assert that God does not play dice with the universe? How do you know that God does not play dice with the universe? How do you know that existence is not just an outrageous run of luck and that in the next moment, this universe, and all you presume, isn't going to go from the Big Bang to a Big Whimper?"

"Or do you really know the mind of God, Dr. Einstein?"

"No, Miss Hornbeck," the scientist mumbled.

"Envy," she said, turning her eyes upon John Lennon. "*Rolling Stone*," she prompted. "Interview," she reminded him. "In which you said in reference to the breakup of the Beatles that you and unnamed others, quote: 'pretty damn well got fed up being sidemen for Paul McCartney,' unquote."

And before John Lennon could defend or deny, she added, almost as an afterthought:

"By the way, Mr. Lennon, has anyone ever tested your boast that the Beatles were 'more popular than Jesus Christ?'"

And although it's probably not what he was thinking, what the ex-Beatle said was: "No, Miss Hornbeck."

"Gentlemen," she said, smiling as sweetly as only a seventh-grade teacher can smile, "nobody questions your accomplishments. All I ask is that you appreciate his."

"Here's a man who came from beginnings as humble as yours, Mr. Lennon, and changed the world as surely as your music. His admirers outnumber the men you commanded in your wars, General; and when it comes to granting insight, the Peterson System is the $E=mc^2$ of natural history.

"He was the heart, the mind, and the soul of an avocation enjoyed by tens of millions, and not an event or adventure within the scope of birding was contemplated that his guidance was not sought.

"But let's dispense with the accolades. Let's just apply the standards of the appeals process. Early admission is granted 'to those individuals who have moved humanity closer to the ideals of heaven and for those to whom respect is due by heaven and earth.' Right?"

The members of the panel nodded.

"Over twenty-five million copies of his book are in print. To what end? Well, consider the environmental movement. A philosophical shift that reversed the centuries-long degradation of Planet Earth, a shift made possible in large part because there was a guide that brought people to intimacy with the natural world. His guide," she said, pointing to Roger.

"You cannot be protective of something you have no intimacy with. It seems clear to me that Roger Peterson helped moved humanity closer to the ideals of heaven.

"Or is there someone here that thinks The Man Upstairs didn't care that one of His favorite planets was getting trashed?"

Nobody did. Great men, whatever their flaws, are respecters of truth.

It was Albert Einstein who spoke for the trio. "You make a good argument, Madam, and I sink maybe you have convinced us. But we can only speak for earth; we are unable to speak for heaven, and zee rules state zat zose seeking early admission must vin zee respect of both . . . "

"That reminds me," she intoned, turning to Roger. "I'm supposed to tell you that you're wanted up on the top floor—following the decision of the panel of course. The guys in scriptures want to kick around the idea of a Field Guide to the Angels, and," she said, pausing, relishing the disclosure, "rumor has it there's a major revision of a very important book in the works. The Man Upstairs would like to hear your thoughts regarding the possibility of a . . . foreword."

It was Albert Einstein who recovered first. "Vell," said the physicist. "It is an honor to velcome you to heaven, Dr. Peterson. Please give my best to zee Boss und now excuse me. Ve all have verk to do und Eternity vaits."

"Welcome to heaven," said Douglas MacArthur, rising, saluting. "Stop by the Officers' Club sometime. Don't just fade away," he said, ignoring his own advice.

"Hey, Birdman," invited John Lennon. "Me and Jimmy Hendrix are jammin' later. You're welcome to sit in. And don't sign anything with those scriptures boys until you talk to my agent. I'll tell him to expect your call."

"Thank you," Roger replied, somewhat taken aback by the sudden turn of events. "And thank you, too, Miss Hornbeck. For everything."

Suddenly, there were lots of other people standing around, offering congratulations. Joe Hickey, Alan Cruickshank, and all the other members of the Bronx County Bird Club.

James Fisher, Rachel Carson, Ludlow Griscom, Maurice Broun, and many other old friends. Everyone had something to say. Everyone had some special occasion to recall. Everyone wanted to be close to the man who had helped move the world just a little closer to the ideal.

It was Angel Bob who had to rein the reunion in, reminding Roger that he was still wanted upstairs. When Roger asked how he was to get there, he was told by a dozen voices:

"Fly."

"I can't fly," Roger insisted to the crowd of amused faces. "I don't have wings."

"But of course you do," counseled James Fisher, reaching around, tugging at what Roger thought was a shirt tail—but wasn't. There in his old traveling companion's hand was the leading edge of a wing.

"But when did I get these?" said an astonished Roger Tory Peterson.

"I told you," said Bob. "You've been growing them all your life. A primary for every accomplishment, a secondary for every generous deed, a covert for every friend."

"Fan 'em, Roger," said Ludlow Griscom. "Let's see the span of your life."

And Roger did. He spread wings that would have put him well up in the record books. If there were record books in heaven. Which, of course, there aren't, because, remember, there is no pride.

But though their length, breadth, and wonderful symmetry were impressive, what most delighted Roger was that when the underwings caught the radiance of heaven, they blazed with yellow shafts of light.

"*Just like the flicker on Old Swede Hill,*" thought Roger. "The one I thought was dead but that was alive!"

As a group, they accompanied Roger to the door, but when they reached the threshold, everyone stepped back. Roger was alone. Before him was Eternity.

He leaned forward. Then he drew back.

He closed his eyes and his will said "jump." But his wings stayed folded and his feet held fast.

"Come on, Roger," his friends encouraged. "Show us your style."

"Try flying like a crow," Joe Hickey suggested, "slow and steady, that's the ticket."

"Or a Peregrine," urged Maurice Broun, "fluid and fast."

"Osprey's more your style, Roger," observed James Fisher. "Just a long soaring glide."

"*Anything* but King Penguin," counseled Ludlow Griscom.

Roger stood, trapped between old friends and endless possibility, frozen like a bird poised for flight.

"All your life, you have only waited for this moment to arrive," he heard himself say. And it was true. But this truth was eclipsed by a greater and more fundamental truth—a truth that lies in all of us.

"I'm afraid," said Roger Tory Peterson. "It's so vast."

Then he felt something. Not a push. Not a shove. Not a bump. More nearly, it was a touch that had in it, the quality of a nudge. It felt for all the world . . .

As if an exploring finger had fallen on his back! Reaching through doubt. Moving him to action. Recalling. For just a moment the time he . . . !

But there was no time for thought. In a blur of motion and light, Roger opened his wings and reached for the horizon.

And as his primaries fused with the air, as his feet broke their bond with the clouds, as he heard the cheers of his friends rise . . . then fall behind, two things suddenly occurred to him:

First, that for the first time in sixty-two years, he'd stood in a crowd, and not a single person had asked him for an autograph.

Second, that since it was heaven, and since he didn't have to watch his diet anymore, he should be on the lookout for a place to stop and get an ice cream cone on his way to meet The Man Upstairs.

"Maybe," he thought, "it would be polite to pick up two."

But the story of the first flight of Roger Tory Peterson is another story for another time. There may be no time in heaven, but this is earth. Where things have a beginning. And things have an end.

Where lives go on, until they become legacies.

Where stories go on, until they stop.

And where tomorrow, if we are lucky, we will all be granted one more opportunity to bring the world a little bit closer to the ideal.

Meet the New Age . . .

It wasn't yet time to start the meeting of the Intragalactic Bird Club. Members were studying data on the projector wall, arguing the merits of the most recent proposed changes in the Cottonwood Flycatcher Complex—Aspen Flycatcher (only recently split from Poplar Flycatcher) to be resplit into two new species: Big Tooth Aspen and Quaking Aspen Flycatcher.

"When were tissue samples from the type specimens placed in cryogenic suspension?" a club elder wanted to know.

"Only eight hundred years ago."

"Fresh," the elder observed, nodding.

"Who did the field work?"

"Two teams—one from Split and Polish Avian Adventurers, Inc., the other from Twitchers Unlimited."

"Hmmm!" mused the club elder. "Can't argue with those credentials."

"Gentlemen!" said a cheerful man (named Harry) who approached the group with a young girl in tow. "I'd like you to meet my niece, Elizabeth."

"Hell-O E-liz-a-Beth," the group harmonized, using the patronizing tones adults employ when dealing with children.

"Hello," responded Elizabeth.

"Elizabeth is interested in birds," Harry added.

"Wonderful!" said the club president. "What field? Harmonic signatures, reptilian divergence?"

"Identification," she replied.

"Ah!" the club president intoned, casting a sly glance around the room. "Care to help us out here?" he nodded toward the projector wall. "We're trying to identify this bird."

Elizabeth squinted at the screen. Turned. Screwed up her face the way children do when adults say something stupid, and said: "There's no bird there."

"Of course there is, dear. Right there. In plain numbers and formulas."

Elizabeth turned to her uncle Harry, sighed audibly, and shook her head.

"Elizabeth doesn't identify birds using formulas," Uncle Harry explained. "She does it by looking at them."

"Looking at what?"

"Looking at birds."

"Looking at birds' what? Chemical composition? Internal parasite complex?"

"Just looking at them," she declared. "I see the bird and identify it."

The club looked mystified.

"No kidding," Harry explained. "The kid goes outside. Finds a bird. Then she has this formula she's developed that helps her identify it. She took me outside and showed me."

"You went outside?" one of the elders asked.

"Uh-huh."

"And there were birds out there?"

"Think so. Small feathered creatures that fly. Elizabeth says that's what they are. She showed me several birds and identified them using a technique that relies on . . . What did you call them, Elizabeth?"

"Key marks," she said. "'cause they hold the key to the identity."

"Can you give us an example?"

"Well, there's one bird that's real common. It's all dark above and orange below, and it eats worms. Know what that is?" she challenged.

Everyone shrugged.

"It's the Rusty-breasted Bird."

The group exchanged uncomprehending glances.

"I did a little research," Harry added. "Concluded that a bird that ate primarily worms would necessarily have had a high percentage of recombinant earthworm proteins in its chemical structure. The most likely candidate is a member of the American Robin complex. If you check the ancient literature, there is, in fact, reference to a bird called 'Robin Red-breast.' Tell them about another bird, Elizabeth."

"Well, there's this real pretty bird that's blue and black and white. Its head's pointy and it screams *"Nay, Nay, Nay"* all the time. I call it the 'Blue Nay.'"

"Say," one of more erudite members of the club intoned, "wasn't there an ancient para/semi/demi/suborder of corvids called 'Jay?' And wasn't that a phonetic rendition of their vocalization? Jay? . . . Nay? . . . Could be just a coincidence, but it's pretty close."

"Elizabeth," said the club president, "there are hundreds of thousands of bird species, and many of them are almost identical in their DNA structure. How can you be certain that these two birds are different just by looking at them?"

"'Cause they got different key marks," she explained.

"Hey," a young club member chimed, "you don't suppose that this is how the ancients distinguished birds, do you? I mean, we've always assumed that birding didn't develop until the age of digital recording and computer correlations. But what if humans learned how to identify birds even before the Information Age? What if John James Sibley or Roger Tory Kaufman used a system that employed 'key marks,' like Elizabeth here?"

"Gentlemen," intoned the club president, "if Elizabeth is right, we could be standing on the verge of a revolution in bird study. Imagine being able to go into the field, look at real birds, and identify them using real-time observation and the power of the human mind. Why, it would herald the dawn of a new age. An age of . . . Field Birding!

"Elizabeth," he continued, "could you possibly take some of us outside, show us some birds, and maybe demonstrate your technique?"

"No," she said. "The birds are sleeping now."

"But don't they look the same when they're asleep?"

"Yep, but it's dark, so you can't see them."

The club members exchanged glances. "Oh."

NOTE TO READERS: Years ago I heard, saw, or read a story about a mathematician living in our distant future who stumbled upon a system of numbers' manipulation that could be done (to everyone's astonishment) with a pad and a pencil. I was just curious to see how this theme might play in the birding arena.

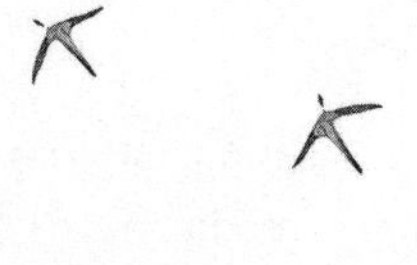

Birdin' in the Rain

The weather forecaster had been predicting rain all week, and he was almost right. It wasn't raining. It was pouring.

"Nobody," I said to my reflection in the windshield, "would be dumb enough to show up for a bird walk in this."

But I was wrong. There, in a parking lot that was more lake than lot, was a single vehicle—a birder too stubborn or naïve to stay in out of the rain.

I moored my car. Took a deep breath. Waded to the back of the vehicle. Popped the hatch and, using what scant protection it offered, I started tugging on wellies (trying all the while to ignore the cold, wet rivulet that was pioneering a channel down the back of my neck).

It was at this sublime moment that my yellow-slicker-wrapped patron splashed up for a parley. Leaning forward, directing a stream of water off his sou'wester into my unfooted boot, he said, "You're not going to cancel, are you?"

"No," I replied, emptying the boot. "I like pelagic birding."

This seemed to soothe him. "It's not so bad once you stand out in it a while," he added.

"Mmmm hmmm," I said through pressed lips—a measure taken to keep my mouth from filling with water.

"It could be worse," he continued. "After all, it could be a *cold* rain. Cold rain is much worse than warm rain."

There's nothing to say in the face of such irrefutable testimony, so I said nothing.

"You know," he continued . . . and I did know! Could draw a

line that connected all the banal, rain-related observations he'd already raised to guess what his next utterance would be. Which was:

" . . . birding in the rain isn't so bad. If I had my choice, I would much rather bird in the rain than in a . . ."

Well, not me. I *hate* getting wet. Hate it in a way that makes the hydrophobia of cats look like the aqua-equanimity of seals. While others get to conduct their birding in places like southeastern Arizona and southern California, I seem always fated to forage in places like . . .

Sitkagi Beach, coastal Alaska—a geographic blotter that absorbs 160 inches of rain, sleet, or snow a year (usually all three at once). In 1982 I was conducting a spring hawk count there, and I'd been warned to buy the best weather gear I could find.

Accordingly, I went down to the local yachting store. I bought the most expensive, most sophisticated "weather gear" on the rack. Decked out in this techweenie-wonder, I could have walked into any yacht club anywhere in the world and been ushered to the best seat at the bar.

I don't know what "weather gear" is supposed to do. One thing it doesn't do is shed water. Fifteen minutes after our bush plane dropped us off on Sitkagi Beach, I was soaked down to my polypros. I stayed that way for ten cold, miserable days.

When I got home, I wrote a scathing letter to the manufacturers of the "Ultimate Weather Gear," who promptly wrote back, explaining that my product was clearly defective, and sent me a replacement.

The replacement proved just as "defective."

I recall a very wet, spring, waterfowl field trip at (then) Brigantine National Wildlife Refuge that occupied a single day in March—but seemed to last forty days and forty nights. There were at least thirty cars in the caravan. Coleader Pete Bacinski and I spent the day walking up and down the line, pointing out rain-grayed duck silhouettes to a host of birders who were, I say with great admiration, too intelligent to get out of their cars.

And few who participated will ever forget the 1998 World Series of Birding—a day that was likened by one surviving team captain to "birding in a car wash."

Ten inches of rain were recorded at our dawn site that day (most of it in the two hours we lingered there). I had three excellent rain suits in my kit—two of which were sodden by 5:00 A.M. I didn't bother putting on the third. What was the point?

The weather was *so* bad, that some of the world's finest waterproof binoculars fogged internally. *So* bad that when teammate Rick Radis's Leica spotting scope was slammed to a dock by the wind, popped off the tripod, plopped in the water, and started bobbing out to sea, I simply walked away.

It was raining too hard to see anything, anyway.

You say that you've been wet, too? You say you fail to see how I've been singled out for water torture? Well, have you ever been to Alice Springs, heart of the desert, Australia? A place whose average annual rainfall is, oh, a trace? I have. Once. Leading a birding trip.

It rained.

So maybe now you'll be able to appreciate why I was brought to interrupt my rain-slickered patron in the middle of his philosophical rubric concerning the merits of birding in the wind vs. rain. Maybe now you can understand why my leader-equanimity slipped its mooring. Why my head snapped up. Why I silenced him with a glance. Why I said in a slow, even monotone: "You aren't about to tell me how you 'would rather bird in the rain than the wind,' are you?"

"Uh-huh," he said.

"If you say it, so help me, I'll drown you," I promised. "Let's go."

We stayed out a full two hours. We didn't see a single bird we couldn't have seen from shore—wherever that was.

A Life without Birding?

It came to me by degrees that my mouth was open. That my mind was blank. That an audience of teenaged faces was turned my way and that some response was needed.

"Excuse me?" I said, to buy time.

"I said, 'What would you be if you weren't a birder?'" the young man repeated, and once again my mind tried to link his question to a response—and failed.

I don't lack for imagination. I just have difficulty coming to grips with inconceivable things—like "nonentity" or "a delicious fat-free diet." To my mind, not being a birder is tantamount to not being.

I bird, therefore I am.

But I did my best. Took his question and turned it upon my life with Socratic intent.

What would I be . . . if a neighborhood chum's grandparents hadn't given her binoculars and a bird book for her ninth birthday? And if, among all the houses in the neighborhood, she hadn't run breathlessly to ours. And if she hadn't said, "Let's go on a bird hike."?

What would I be . . . if those World War II binoculars hadn't lived in my father's dresser? Or if he hadn't trusted me to use them? Or if an overbearing parental concern had prevented me from wandering bird-filled woodlands at will where I was brought to discover life's greatest discovery, which is . . . discovery itself?

Or what would I be . . . if warblers hadn't made treetops come alive in spring? If cardinals and Blue Jays never brought animation and color to winter? If the promise of Wood Ducks and kingfishers didn't lie around every bend?

Or if, in college, when I was hardly older than the students facing me now, the personal effects of a late, favorite uncle had not included *A Field Guide to the Birds*—and the tacit message, ferried to a young adult seeking identity, that *bird watching wasn't just a childhood fancy, bird watching was something that could anchor an adult lifetime, too?* Anyone's life!

Including mine.

But how was I going to explain all this to the earnest young man who had formulated a simple question and wanted only a simple answer?

"What would I be," I repeated to those earnest young eyes, "if I weren't a birder?"

He nodded.

"Dead," I said. "Any other questions?"

Another hand went up.

"Yes," I said.

"Do you think you'll ever include us in an essay?"

"Maybe," I replied.

Understanding Wren

I think that I could understand all if I understood wren. All the contradictions that puzzle me. All the answers that have eluded me. All the hopes and what-ifs and do-you-supposes, all the things that truly matter. If only I could understand wren.

In my backyard (the one surrounded on four sides by the rest of the world, the same world that borders yours), I sit and do the opposite of concentrate. Purging my mind of uncut grass and porches in need of painting. Thinking that leftovers will be fine for dinner so long as I am left to contemplate wren.

Small and brown, solitary and furtive. Given to small rages when cat appears but more often to song—a wonderful, cascading, rise and fall of notes that knit heaven and earth.

Now, in summer, with a nest filled with young, wren has less time for song, even less time for me. But I try to catch him between trips to the nest box. Toss questions his way, hoping one will give him pause. There are things I need to know, things fundamentally simple that only wren might be ken to.

I want to know, what is the advantage of small in a world full of peril? I was told that safety and security meant being big, not being wren; or if you couldn't be big, be many. Safety lies in numbers. Stay with the herd. That's what I was told.

But small suits wren. And the term "flock" does not exist even as a concept in the mind of wren.

I want to know, why shy and brown? I was led to believe that to be successful you had to stand out. Be an achiever. Turn heads. Be the hit of the party. Be . . .

Anything but wren.

I want to know why a small, solitary, furtive, brown bird has such a big voice—or is this why?

And how a bird that sings so wonderfully can pierce the eggs of rivals—even the eggs of other birds—when bird populations are high and food in short supply. (Is it right that a bird that sings so beautifully should kill so freely?)

Is it?

And if there is, behind those small, black eyes of wren, a mind that reasons, what is the reason?

I want to know. Because if I had these answers, I think that I might understand all. If not all, then at least more. And if not more, then at least, wren.

Which is more than I understand now.

A Chat about the Rules

I halved the distance and stopped. The Yellow-breasted Chat didn't fly. I cut the distance to ten feet . . . five! The bird wouldn't budge.

This is incredible, I thought. All my life, birds have fled as I approached. This one was breaking the bird vs. birder rules. This one was letting me so close I couldn't even focus on it.

"Close enough?" the bird asked.

"YOU CAN TALK!" I exclaimed.

"I'm a chat. What'd you expect? And you're the guy who writes that bird-watching column, right?"

I nodded.

"Excellent," replied the bird. "I've got a message for your readers. A sort of warning peck across the bow. Tell your birding confederates to stop changing the rules, or we're going to stop playing fair."

"Excuse me?" I said.

"Look. We worked the rules of engagement out a long time ago," the bird explained. "We hide; you try to find us. We offer brief or distant looks; you try to note field marks. We fly away; you guess our name. Get it right, you win."

"So?" I questioned.

"So stop with all this digital recording equipment and video stuff. That's not field birding. That's collecting, then making identifications after the fact. And that's not fair," the bird said mildly. "Real birding in real time. That's what we agreed to."

The bird had a point. Field identification is a real-time deductive process that brings knowledge and experience to bear *in the field*. The art has taken a century to develop, and it is the very essence of birding.

Hooking a camcorder up to a spotting scope for later review is the very antithesis of field birding. It doesn't require skill. It doesn't constitute a challenge. All it requires is a good library or a skilled second party to identify the bird for you.

Still, I couldn't see where it made much difference, and I couldn't see what the birds were going to do about advances in technology anyway—a point that I pointed out.

The chat smiled. "Watch," it said, and I did. Watched as the bird pulled out a stretchy red cap. Dabbed a little makeup over his lores. Garnished the tip of his tail with a strategic squirt of guano . . . and suddenly I was looking at a newly minted Fan-tailed Warbler.

"You can't do that," I whispered.

"Au contraire," he replied, removing the cap, reaching for a comb, parting his crown. Then, fluffing his back feathers, he reached for a mascara kit, etched a black V on his chest, then started on his face.

"You want Eastern or Western Meadowlark?" he asked.

"It's not fair!" I croaked.

"Exactly right," the bird pronounced.

"It's going to make every identification questionable!" I gasped.

"Worse than that," the bird said. "It's going to make Life Birds cheap. As we speak, fifty million American Robins are learning to spin like tops, just waiting for the signal to bob their tails and drop into the nearest birdbath. How much do you think your Life Red Phalarope is going to be worth when that happens?

"It gets worse," he continued cheerfully. "All across North America, squadrons of House Sparrows are hoarding yellow Easter-egg dye, bleaching their undertail coverts and training for life in the canopy. It won't be long before a birder won't cross the street to see a Bachman's Warbler.

"It doesn't have to be this way," the bird promised. "Just stick to the status quo, leave the techie gadgetry at home, we'll forget about the charades. Deal?"

I said I'd think about it and started to leave. But then it occurred to me that bird photography broke the real-time rule, too. Birds had let us get away with that. I turned to ask for a rule interpretation only to find a Labrador Duck perched where the chat had been. As I watched, the bird threw back its head, sang *witchity, witchity, witchity*, then *Oh, sweet Canada, Canada, Canada*, and winked.

I turned and ran.

Passing the Pen

This essay is about nature writing and columnists. It is also about two men. One is Roger Barton; the other is Ned Smith. Both are dead. But having come to the full span of their lives is not the only thing these gentlemen have in common.

Both were writers of columns on natural history. Mr. Barton's column was entitled "Outdoors with Roger Barton," and from 1947 to 1972 it appeared in the *Newark Sunday News*. Ned Smith's chronicle, dubbed "Gone for the Day," was a regular feature in *Pennsylvania Game News*, the magazine of the Pennsylvania Game Commission.

You may never have read either man's column. But if you are a regular reader of my writings, then you have been touched by theirs. These writers influenced me before I was a writer. Their thoughts live in my thoughts and my pen is an extension of theirs.

I call Roger Barton "Mr. Barton" for two reasons. First, we never met, and this binds me to a measure of formality. Second, during the years I used to run into the house and leaf through the pages of the Sunday news until I found "Outdoors with Roger Barton," I was a child. Everyone was a Mr. back then (or a Mrs. or a Miss), and memory keeps them that way today.

It is unfortunate that we never did meet, because our common ground is immense. Not only was Roger Barton an enthusiastic birder, but also he was, in his time, president of the organization I have worked for since 1976—the New Jersey Audubon Society. When he retired from his job in a New York advertising firm, he and his wife moved to a farm in Hunterdon County—as the crow flies about five miles from the farm that my wife, Linda, and I lived on from 1987 to 1991.

But the point is that even though we never met to discuss our common point of reference, we did have one very important thing in common: *his column*. I lived it—as much as I lived for the natural world. It put me in touch with someone who shared my interest. He was, except for a childhood chum, the only other birder I had any dealings with, and his column was our bond.

Then, one day, something happened that transformed the vicarious relationship I had with Roger Barton, something that brushed me with the social network that would become woven into the fabric of my life.

My father, my brother, and I were driving to visit cousins who lived south of Morristown. We passed a pond, on James Street, just down the street from Thomas Jefferson School.

The pond and the school are still there, in case you're curious.

As we went by, I noticed that a tall, all-white bird was standing in the pond. *An egret!* I knew it instantly (although I'd never seen one before). "An egret!" I shouted—but I didn't ask my father to stop. Just seeing a bird so rare was treasure enough.

The bird with the snowy plumes, the bird with the "golden slippers." I'd seen them in books. Now I'd seen one for real.

Two weeks later, in his column, Roger Barton dutifully noted the sighting of a snowy egret that had been reported to him by a (Mr./Mrs./Miss) Somebody or Other. The bird was the same bird I'd seen in the Jefferson School Pond.

I think my heart stopped. I think I read the words a dozen times. I cut that column out and saved it, proof positive that the vision had been real, that my identification had been correct. And that something I'd witnessed was significant enough to be written about in a newspaper.

I think I am correct when I say that that innocuous observation, reported by a dutiful columnist, to an unknown reader, changed my life. I have Roger Barton to thank for this—and for impressing upon me the power and influence of the written word.

Roger Barton was an imposing-looking gentleman—if the photo on the dust jacket of his long-out-of-print book *Confessions of a Bird Watcher* does him justice. The portrait shows a square-jawed man with a direct gaze. It recalls Dwight D. Eisenhower.

Ned Smith, on the other hand, was a slight, slim man with pixie features and a frock of hair that seemed ruled by whimsy. We met on the Hawk Watch platform in Cape May Point State Park in the fall of 1978. He introduced himself, and I asked if he was the same Ned Smith who wrote "Gone for the Day." He said he was and seemed pleased that I was familiar with it.

I was more than familiar. During my adolescent years, the column was my bible, and the man who wrote it, my idol. I told him so.

Ned Smith was a quiet man, maybe a shy man, and like many quiet people, he had much to say, particularly about the natural world. His column consisted of diary entries, and they related the observations and musings of this great, great student of nature.

He wandered, as I wandered, putting himself in the path of miracles that sometimes happen—a grouse that flushes, a weasel that runs across your path, a raccoon draped across a limb, or a goshawk dashing through the trees. These were the grist of his mill.

He was a good, clear-thinking writer and a marvelous artist. His sketches graced his column, and his art often found a place on the cover of *Pennsylvania Game News*. And he was, I came to know later in my life, an avid hawk watcher—a patron of Hawk Mountain, Pennsylvania, and a frequent visitor to Cape May Point where I worked (and still do).

In 1984 our lives were joined by a more-than-shared interest, friendship, or writer-reader bond. In October of that year, Hawk Mountain Sanctuary held a celebration to commemorate its fiftieth anniversary. I was the Friday night speaker. Ned Smith was the artist for the commemorative poster.

It was a stunning poster showing two Golden Eagles, an adult and an immature, navigating the crest of the North Lookout as the afternoon sun set their hackles ablaze. The poster, properly framed, sits on the wall of my office. It is beautiful. It has outlived the words of that Friday night speech and Ned Smith, too.

At the beginning of this essay, I said it would be about nature writing and columnists. I'll keep my promise and get to the heart of it. All over North America, in small towns and large cities, there are people like Roger Barton and Ned Smith, people who write columns about birds and nature. Hundreds of them. They aren't paid very much, these columnists. Some, in fact, are not paid at all.

But they perform a very important service. They reach out, just as Roger Barton and Ned Smith did, and touch people just like you and me. These columns draw even the most stay-at-home, don't-care-to-socialize people into a network of kindred spirits, uniting them by shared interest and the written word.

These nature writers are gurus and tribal leaders. They are sometimes information nerve centers when a rare bird is seen, and they are the people who get calls late in the night from a reader who is having trouble identifying some bird that is coming to the feeder "that looks a lot like a House Finch but . . ."

They have a great deal of responsibility and this is why: The U.S. Fish and Wildlife Service estimates that over 70,000,000 U.S. residents are interested in birds. This is indeed a lot of people, and I am certain that you and I were included.

The American Birding Association, North America's largest birding organization, has only about 25,000 members. The best-selling bird-watching magazine on the racks has a subscription of less than 200,000.

So how do the rest of the many millions of people who are interested in birds get their news about birds? Many, probably most, get it the way I did—back when I would run into the house with the Sunday paper or listen to the sound of the mailman and hope that another *Pennsylvania Game News* had arrived. They get it from the Roger Bartons and Ned Smiths of the world and maybe those writers who were inspired by these great writers and who now know the great joy and great responsibility that comes from reaching out and touching others with their words and their pens.

Because who knows? Somewhere among the ranks of readers, there may be a future writer, reading these words, right now. One who will pick up the pen and wield it for all those writers who came before, then hold it in trust for those who come after.

The Perfect Bird

As one who made his appearance at the tail end of creation, I wasn't around when the folks in R&D designed birds. All in all a splendid job, but despite their many achievements, they failed in one stupendous regard.

They failed to design the perfect bird.

Accordingly, and just in case creation is recast, I would like to submit the following traits and characteristics which taken in sum would make . . .

The "Perfect Bird." That's its common name. Easy to say, easy to remember. In Latin, it's the same: *Avis perfectus.* No subspecies. How can you have gradations of perfection?

The Perfect Bird is the size of a turkey and has the wingspan of an eagle, the legs of a crane, the feet of a moorhen, and the talons of a Great-horned Owl. It eats kudzu, surplus zucchini, and feral cats, and has been known to predate upon home owners who fire up their lawn mowers before 7:00 A.M. on the weekend.

The bill is unmistakable, combining the shape of Roseate Spoonbill, the pattern of Atlantic Puffin, and the extended lower mandible of Black Skimmer (except it appears to be the upper mandible because the bill is crossed).

Of course it has a crest.

Of course it has a long, forked tail.

Males and females are identical and have an overall plumage pattern of a drake Wood Duck *except that* the Perfect Bird also has golden ear tufts (like a Horned Grebe), the azure-colored eye of a Flightless Cormorant, the bill color of a Caspian Tern (same color as the gular sacs of displaying males), the gorget of a Magnificent Hummingbird, the wing pattern of an Ivory-billed Woodpecker, cerulean upperparts, vermillion underparts, and the tail pattern of an American Redstart (replicated on both tines). Everything is iridescent, and it glows in the dark.

Did I forget to mention the ruby crown and the red epaulets?

Well, it's got them.

The song is rich and varied, combining the quality of a Wood Thrush with the volume of a Screaming Piha and a range that goes from Ruffed-Grouse-drumroll low to Ruby-crowned-Kinglet high. An accomplished mimic, it sings the entire songs (not just snatches or phrases) of the world's most-celebrated songbirds, plus all of Jimmy Buffet's songs and Fleetwood Mac's greatest hits, in addition to "Layla," "Freebird," "Inagodadavida," Bing Crosby's "White Christmas," and "God Bless America" in stereo. Songs are usually sung in commercial-free, seven-song sets.

Between sets, and for the sake of identification, it calls its name.

Loudly.

The Perfect Bird is also an accomplished aerialist. It can outpace swifts in level flight, outstoop a Peregrine, outmaneuver swallows, hover, kite, and even backstroke. In migration, following a route that customarily circumnavigates the globe in a polar orbit, it flies in a diagnostic "P" (for "Perfect").

Or would, if and when enough birds could be mustered for a quorum. Needless to say, the Perfect Bird is also extremely rare. Only you and birders who have Sir Galahad's blood running undiluted in their veins have ever seen one, and the bird is invisible to anyone whose Life List exceeds your own.

Despite all its stunning visual and auditory attributes, the bird is uncommonly shy and retiring. Most observers gain little more than a tantalizing glimpse that makes them ache with longing for the rest of their lives, which is, in the case of most observers, short. The burden of knowing that the chances of ever seeing the Perfect Bird again is almost zero drives many to suicide.

You, however, know that the Perfect Bird is also extremely vain, and so realize that the species can be lured from cover by training your binoculars on the spot where the bird is hiding (designated, for your eyes only, by a large, fluorescent, orange bull's-eye superimposed over the foliage). Seeing its reflection in the objective lens, the Perfect Bird will approach to a distance equal to the minimum close focus of your instrument and begin to display.

How the Perfect Bird is able to know what binocular you are using remains a mystery.

While it only appears just when things seem hopeless and you are on the verge of giving up the search, the Perfect Bird will remain in perfect view and in good light until you go blind or decide to wander off and find a chickadee or titmouse.

Of course, any sighting of a Perfect Bird requires thorough documentation. The Perfect Bird submits its own Rare Bird Sighting report to the proper state records committee, complete with perfectly focused, point-blank photos of you standing with your arm around the bird and your calendar wristwatch (showing the time and the date) displayed. Photos are personalized and autographed by the Perfect Bird.

And in case you are worrying about the photos ever being dated by the well-considered decisions of committees dealing with classification and nomenclature, relax. The name will never be changed. Never. The Perfect Bird will never be split. It will never be renamed the Common Perfect Bird, the Northern Perfect Bird, or Cordilleran Perfect Bird. Its name will never be modified by so much as a hyphen.

The Perfect Bird is, by its nature, the Perfect Bird. Who's going to mess with perfection?